Life and Teaching of Two Immortals

Volume I: Kou Hong

Jeff Kottkamp) Lt Gov. of FL

Life and Teaching of Two Immortals

Volume I: Kou Hong

By Master
NI, HUA-CHING

The Shrine of the Eternal Breath of Tao
College of Tao & Traditional Chinese Healing
SANTA MONICA

Acknowledgements: Thanks and appreciation to Suta Cahill and Janet DeCourtney for typing, proofreading, editing and typesetting this book.

The Shrine of the Eternal Breath of Tao,
Malibu, California 90265

College of Tao and Traditional Chinese Healing,
1314 Second Street #A
Santa Monica, California 90401

Library of Congress Catalog Card Number 91-62058
ISBN 0-937064-47-5

Library of Congress Cataloging-in-Publication Data

Ni, Hua-Ching.
  Life and teaching of two immortals / by Ni, Hua-Ching.
    p.   cm.
  Contents: v. 1. Kou Hong.
  ISBN 0-937064-47-5 (pbk. : v. 1) : $12.95
    1. Spiritual life (Taoism) 2. Ko, Hung, 284-364. 3. Ch'en T'uan, ca. 885-989. I. Title.
  BL1923.N538 1992
  299'.514448–dc20

                                 91-62058
                                     CIP

This book is dedicated
to those who pursue the subtle reality of life
which is not confined or limited
by the physical form of life.

Master Kou Hong

Contents

To female readers,

According to natural spiritual teaching, male and female are equally important in the natural sphere. This is seen in the diagram of Tai Chi. Thus, discrimination is not practiced in our tradition. All my work is dedicated to both genders of human people.

Wherever possible, constructions using masculine pronouns to represent both sexes are avoided; where they occur, we ask your tolerance and spiritual understanding. We hope that you will take the essence of my teaching and overlook the superficiality of language. Gender discrimination is inherent in English; ancient Chinese pronouns do not have differences of gender. I wish for all of you achievement above the level of language or gender.

Thank you, H. C. Ni

Prelude

The Integral Way is the destination of all religions, while it leaves behind all religions just like the clothing of different seasons and different places. The Natural Subtle Truth is the goal of serious science, but it leaves behind all sciences as a partial and temporal description of the Integral Truth.

The teaching of the Integral Way includes all religious subjects, yet it is not on the same level as religions. Its breadth and depth go far beyond the limits of religion. The teaching of the Subtle Essence serves people's lives like religions do, yet it transcends all religions and contains the essence of all religions.

The teaching of the Integral Way is not like any of the sciences. It is above the level of any single subject of science.

The teaching of the Integral Way is the master teaching of all. However, it does not mean the teaching relies on a master. It means the teaching of the Subtle Universal Essence is like a master key which can unlock all doors leading to the Unified Subtle Truth. It teaches or shows the truth directly. It does not stay on the emotional surface of life or remain at the level of thought or belief. Neither does it stay on the intellectual level of life, maintaining skepticism and searching endlessly. The teaching of the Subtle Essence presents the core of the subtle truth and helps you reach it yourself.

Preface

In spiritual learning, if your purpose is to look for spiritual development, it is important to know the right school. Otherwise, seriousness would cause you to misuse the opportunity of a lifetime as you applied yourself diligently to the wrong learning. The real teaching of the Subtle Truth has no stiffening external style to choose from, like restaurants that offer different "cuisine." It teaches the true knowledge of food and cooking in order to give you real benefit, instead of only pleasing your palate. This is the fundamental difference. Lao Tzu said the teaching of the Integral Way is like unspiced food; although it does not appeal to your taste buds, it is more nutritious. (Chapter 35 of the *Tao Teh Ching.*)

The Subtle Essence is the spirituality of the universe and of mankind. It is too subtle to describe; you can only learn it through self-spiritual cultivation with the guidance I have offered. Yet, in the describable level, you can learn about it from the comparative study of the existing examples - the religions. In my work I frequently make use of them and comment about them to achieve this purpose. However, only a few classics such as those by Lao Tzu and Chuang Tzu discussed the Subtle Essence. In these two volumes, I make a new attempt.

In later times and later generations, the teaching of the Subtle Essence became blended with or was being used to support the establishment of religion. As a result, however, the teaching of spiritual truth was contorted and could not be maintained as the open and broad spiritual education for all people. Religions do not teach enlightenment; they teach different types of practices which have other purposes and functions.

Aside from following religions which are very easy to contact, you might be interested in doing your own spiritual development. Spiritual development is more important than political or social independence. You do not allow anybody else to manage your life, in things as small as spending money, so why allow religions or anybody else to manage this essential part of your life spiritually?

This book, *The Life and Teaching of Two Immortals*, has been divided into two volumes which present Master Kou Hong and Master Chen Tuan respectively. These two individuals had spiritual interest and years of cultivation and achievement. They may serve as the good model for spiritual students and teachers.

Master Kou Hong is around 1,700 years ahead of us, and Master Chen Tuan is around 1,000 years ahead. They are both models of spiritual development that can serve to inspire us. About half of the material that each master taught was for enlightenment and wisdom. The other half was useful and effective spiritual practices which could bring about a result different from what religions teach. These practices, when applied to a healthy life, can lead a person to complete development of oneself as a human individual. The lives of these two great teachers expressed that they were completely developed, balanced individuals. Balance is an important part of a healthy personality. Each individual is born with self nature; self nature is the spiritual nature of people. This is the common reality of the existence of every person and thing in the universe, yet the approach to realize one's spiritual self nature can take one of two main ways. One way is to cultivate one's spirit in solitude. This way holds the belief that mingling with general society is akin to murdering one's own spiritual nature. This way encourages people to leave society and become hermits. In solitude, no self is displayed, which brings great spiritual enjoyment. The other way of realizing oneself is to cultivate one's spirit through social work or worldly activity. This way encourages people to become great leaders or helpers of society. In a group of people, one is constantly aware of the self. This brings the need for constant refinement and improvement.

Both Master Kou Hong and Chen Tuan had strong spiritual interest to begin their lives. Both extended the range of their lives to include each of the two ways to spiritual achievement, spiritual enjoyment and worldly service. During their lives, they responded to what was needed in the world. Both were engaged in war. Kou Hong went to war to set an example of minimizing killing to restore the order in society. Chen Tuan was famous for his "sleeping." In his "sleep," he extended himself to the activity of restoring peace in a society with restless military competition of the warlords. He achieved providing people with a chance to rest, be safe and find a new life with better opportunity, and ended a 52-year span of turmoil in society.

After settling down the world in a certain good order, both Masters Chen Tuan and Master Kou Hong taught in their own informal schools. Both directed their teachings for open spiritual achievement rather than promoting a rigid religion to promote themselves as leaders of society. Their model of life greatly impressed my young heart; thus, it was my choice to continue their teaching. I like to live a life of spiritual enjoyment away from all kinds of possible disturbance, but I also respond to the world's problems in my time. I preserve and revive all the truly beneficial teachings and achievements of different generations for people who need to stabilize their spiritual position to live in a new time, a new world that has all kinds of new thoughts and new confusion.

In the book of Master Kou Hong, there is one chapter of philosophical material. Although it is not directly Kou Hong's teaching, it is also Kou Hong's spirit to offer guidance appropriate to all times and all places.

In the book of Master Chen Tuan, there are two chapters of philosophical material. Before Chen Tuan, or at the time of Chen Tuan, Chinese scholars focused on the pursuit of governmental positions to share ruling power over ordinary people. Master Chen Tuan's philosophical influence on Chinese scholars was to change their focus from seeking position and fame to searching for spiritual truth. Although the material in these two chapters was not written directly by him, it reflects Master Chen Tuan's philosophical orientation which helped the scholars to open up. New inspiration came to them when they studied the old inspiration of the Subtle Essence.

It was a great happiness for scholars and teachers in different generations to rediscover the Subtle Essence, which is related to their own eternal life. Although some of this material may be different from what you are accustomed to, and hard to digest or understand all at once, I hope you have patience with it and read several lines, several paragraphs or several pages at one time. Reread these books or parts if necessary. I am sure you will be rewarded by your efforts, and hope that you will find these two books enjoyable and helpful.

Sincerely,
Your Spiritual Friend
Ni, Hua-Ching

Chapter 1

The Versatile Master of Natural Spiritual Truth: Kou Hong

I

Pau Po Tzu, which means "the one who embraces the simple essence," is the pen name of Master Kou Hong. Kou Hong was born around 283 A.D. He ascended in 363 A.D. (Some say he was born around 284 A.D. and ascended in 364 A.D.) In his old age, Kou Hong lived in West Lake, which is in the Kou Mountain Range. It was here that he accomplished his cultivation. With his literary training and Confucian education, he laid down the basic foundation for the teaching of spiritual truth in later generations. He was also a healer in Traditional Chinese Medicine and a specialist in the art of refining medicines, including immortal medicine.

Kou Hong was born in Tanyan, which is now Chiang Su province. Kou Hong was the grand nephew of Master Kou Shuan. When he was young, he worked hard at his scholastic pursuits, but his deepest interest and wish was his own self-development and the attainment of spiritual immortality. Kou Hong learned from Master Cheng Shih Yuan, the student of his great uncle Master Kou Shuan, who taught him the method of refining medicine, both internally and externally.

Kou Hong had another name, Young River, which means "a river that just started." Chinese scholars usually had two or more names: one is more formal, while the other is a kind of literary title for personal enjoyment. The latter is not a nickname, but a scholastic name.

Kou Hong's book, *Pau Po Tzu*, recorded his use of minerals to refine certain medicines and described the way to refine base metals into precious metals. He also wrote how to use herbs to cure diseases. He made a certain contribution to the fields of chemistry and medicine. In his book, he also wrote about spiritual immortality, possible negative spiritual influences, the elixir for immortality and how to use spiritual practice to avoid evil and disasters.

Some scholars have confirmed the value of those practices, but others have not; yet the teaching was given to all.

Kou Hong also wrote a book called The Formula behind the Elbow. In ancient times, people wore clothing with big sleeves. Sometimes there was a little pocket on the inside of the sleeve behind the elbow. Master Kou Hong carried there a secret book that he wrote that is of great value in Chinese medicine.

Kou Mountain, next to West Lake of Huangchow in Chekiang Province, was so named because Master Kou Hong lived and refined his golden immortal medicine there. Kou Mountain is north of West Lake, between the Mountain of Precious Stone and the Mountain of Golden Clouds at Sunset. This area covers a number of square miles. On top of the mountain was a terrace where he stayed to refine his internal medicine and a well whose waters he used for refining external medicine to help the internal medicine. On the top of this mountain was a high spot built up by stones where he had a hut. That spot was called Chu Yang Tai, which could be translated as "the terrace of welcoming the morning sun." It is one of the ten scenic spots of West Lake, and is a lovely place for enjoying an early morning sunrise.

Because he lived in West Lake quite long, people who lived near West Lake and knew him missed him when he did not live there. These years are not described in his personal biography, which does not give complete details about many years of his life. Later, I would like to tell you the foundation of his life and background; it will be helpful to your understanding.

All around West Lake are mountains, high and low. People can walk on them in many places, and look all around to enjoy the view. They are magnificent mountains. Kou Mountain is between the two high peaks of the South and North. There are many spots not as great as Kou Mountain but which are nevertheless special places. In China, places are typically given names according to their shape, but Kou Mountain was named after Kou Hong because he cultivated and achieved himself there. The special person made this place well known.

Kou Hong was originally from the city of Gi Yung in Chin Ling region. Ging Ling became the capital city in the South, and has since changed names to Nan Ching (the Southern capital.) This is at the southern end of the Yangtze River in the territory of Chiang Su province. During the time of the three kingdoms, his great uncle, Kou Shuan (or Kou Hsiao-Hsieng) followed Master Tzo Tzu who was *BK* famous for magic power, and received from him the special spiritual book called *The Book of Nine Golden Elixirs.*

Master Kou Shuan ascended during the daytime. On the day he ascended, important books like the book of top purity (the *Book of Three Caves*) became known as precious spiritual treasures which tell the way to reach alliance with the spiritual realm. Those books helped make people interested in spiritual learning. He gave that book and all other important spiritual books to his student Cheng Shih Yuan. He told him that in the future, one of his descendants would be a realizer of the Integral Way, and that he must not keep the secret from him. This was a prophesy about the future achievement of his grand nephew, the young Kou Hong.

The birth of Kou Hong was common or ordinary. His father and mother died early, so he was very poor. Fortunately, he did not care about fame or wealth; he was happy with an ordinary life. He had no interest in worldly desires. He loved to read books and inquire about the subtle truth of life. He did not have many books to read, so he would go to the mountain to cut wood and sell it. With this money he bought paper, brush and ink and he borrowed other people's books and copied them to read. As he made the copy, at the same time he studied it. Kou Hong was not afraid of cold or hot weather; he constantly studied no matter what the weather. By doing this, after more than ten years, he became a knowledgeable scholar.

Someone recognized the high level of his knowledge and told him, "If you were to attain a governmental position, you would not need to worry about poverty." To which Kou Hong replied, "I study for the sake of my personal understanding of the subtle law, not for position, fame or wealth." His friend continued to argue with him, saying, "It is all right to be without name and position, but how can you live in poverty? You are young and unmarried. Without a government position, how will you support a wife and children?" Kou Hong laughed and replied, "In ancient times, there was a scholar who never become a government official, but he was married. He was almost as poor as I, and was married to a virtuous woman named Mung Guang. This woman especially chose him. No friend could make him trade his knowledge for money or position, so he gave them up." Kou Hong added, "I am just like that man."

Kou Hong's knowledge was high and his understanding was deep, but his interest was not shallow. He would still not be employed by the government. So he closed the door to making friends and became choosy, even about whom he would meet. He preferred solitude to being with friends and avoided worldly life. He always took trips to the mountains and lakes for personal enjoyment. One day, he came to a beautiful green mountain and sat on a white stone under some tall pines. He looked at the aura produced by the mountain and observed that it was not confined to the immediate shape of the mountain but stretched high above the mountain. He thought it curious that the mountain's energy was not immediately seen from far away. The good energy of the mountain is within the mountain. The aura is the same thing as the appearing energy. It is high above, far away, and within the mountain all at the same time. He wondered whether a person who could hold the invisible energy within one's own body could reach internal sufficiency and not need to rely on the energy of the external world.

Kou Hong was sitting there enjoying his thoughts and newly gained understanding that a place can produce energy when someone unexpectedly appeared. This man was Bao Shuan, the governor of the South Sea. He had hiked to the mountain with his ministers and some guests. They had brought wine and food, and had stopped in the gazebo halfway up the mountain. After refreshing themselves with a meal, they all went on a walk. Bao Shuan was walking with one of his friends who had special vision which gave him the ability to know or read people. Seeing Kou Hong sitting nearby, they purposely went over to where he sat. Bao Shuan's friend with special vision could see that the man who was sitting on the white stone had an elegant type of energy. In fact, the Governor and his friend both marveled at Kou Hong's energy and were interested in communicating with him. Bao Shuan said, "Look at that man. His figure is so graceful. He is a person who has much higher energy than that of most people, yet, it seems that he does not have any attendants with him."

The person who had achieved special spiritual vision looked at the governor and said, "I can see that this young man shall have a position, but the position will not be very important. Is there anything special your highness can see about him?"

Bao Shuan said, "I only see that he has the potential to be in a high position if he so chooses, but I cannot see anything else about him."

"Look at the energy in his face between the eye and the eyebrow. He has a special spiritual energy, and his eyes have light. His body is like a wild crane with absolute freedom; he shall become a spiritual immortal in the future," his friend commented.

Bao Shuan listened to what his friend said, but he did not take it in completely. He himself went forward, approaching Kou Hong with a sign of greeting. Kou Hong was still enjoying the energy of the mountain when he heard someone greet him. He immediately stood up and bowed to the older people and said, "Please excuse me, I was just enjoying the beauty of the mountain. I did not know you had come over here. I should not be in your way; I am sorry about that."

Bao Shuan appreciated his politeness and felt a fondness for him. He said, "You look like a nice, intelligent person. You must have an important position in the government. How can you have time to come to the mountain and be alone?"

Kou Hong replied, "As I have heard, even a person with high knowledge who takes a position in government may also have interest in mountains and bodies of water. Although I have achieved nothing and am far from any position of importance, it is healthy to enjoy the good energy of mountains and waters to nurture my spiritual energy."

After hearing this, Bao Shuan became happy. He said, "Not only are your looks above ordinary, but what you are saying is also above ordinary. I admire you. What is your name?"

Kou Hong answered, "I did not yet ask yours. It is difficult for me to introduce myself first." It was an ancient ritual for older or more important people to always introduce themselves first.

Bao Shuan replied, "I am the governor of the region around the South Sea. I am a man who is like the sun that has already passed the point of high noon, nothing worth mentioning."

Kou Hong immediately gave him a bow and said, "Oh, you are as high as the Tai Mountain and as respected as the Northern Star. My name is Kou Hong. I am a simple unachieved scholar. It is a great opportunity for me to see your eminent purple energy." (Purple energy means noble and precious knowledge.)

After hearing the young man's name, Bao Shuan said to him, "Oh, you are Master Kou. I do not know where you live."

Kou Hong answered, "I was born in Gi Yung Chin Ling."

Bao Shuan said, "In the time of the three kingdoms, in Gi Yung, there was an achieved one who ascended to the sun in the bright daytime. His name was Kou Shuan. Your surname is the same; you must know him."

Kou Hong humbly said, "He is my great uncle, but I am not immortal. I am an ordinary mortal." When Bao Shuan heard this, he was happy because he himself was a true realizer of the Integral Way, the student of Mother Chern, the mother of Yellow Altar.

Bao Shuan turned around to this friend who had a special vision and said, "No wonder that you say he too has immortal energy," for his friend had seen that the great uncle and the great nephew had a similar type of energy. His friend was happy that Bao Shuan understood and agreed with him about the special energy of Kou Hong. It is spiritual truth that people are energy, and the differences in their energies is what makes people different from one another. All things in the universe, no matter how solid or nebulous they appear, are just different energies.

Kou Hong heard their conversation and requested an explanation. Bao Shuan told him about the observations his friend had made before they approached him. Kou Hong listened to what they said about how they viewed him, and he modestly denied having high spiritual potential. However, in his mind, he was impressed by their discussion of spiritual immortality. It was clearly something that he was beginning to become interested in.

Because Kou Hong saw that the governor was an important person and had many people following him, he asked to leave his presence. However, Bao Shuan took his hand and asked Kou Hong to tell him exactly where he lived before he would let him say good-bye and leave. Would you like to know why Bao Shuan liked Kou Hong so much? Because he had a daughter whom he loved greatly, and he had not yet found a son-in-law. He had been looking for a suitable young man for a long time. When he met Kou Hong, he could see that the young man was not just an ordinary person, but someone who was talented and who could present himself well.

The next day, Bao Shuan asked his friend to be match-maker and visit Kou Hong. Kou Hong refused the marriage proposal again and again for the reason that he lived in poverty. However, with Bao Shuan's insistence and great sincerity, the marriage agreement was made. After the marriage took place, husband, wife and father-in-law came to appreciate and enjoy each other very much.

Bao Shuan's favorite pastime was the gathering of external medicine, in the form of all types of herbs. He also knew about internal medicine which is a person's internal energy. Because he realized that Kou Hong had not yet learned much about internal energy transformation, even though he was the descendent of a spiritual immortal, Bao Shuan took it upon himself to teach him what he had learned about spiritual refinement. Mornings and evenings, whenever they had time, they studied together.

Bao Shuan asked Kou Hong if he knew his great uncle's secrets of cultivation, because he had heard that they had been passed down. Kou Hong answered, "I have heard that spiritual cultivation depends upon each individual's self-cultivation. Although I learned some techniques or methods as part of the family passage, they were ordinary things like exercise, which can only help to keep my blood circulating and safeguard my health for my old age."

Bao Shuan said, "If you wish to learn to ascend, you must learn the great immortal medicine." Kou Hong agreed with him and paid close attention to learning the high method of refining the great immortal medicine.

II

During the reign of Emperor Cheng Ti of the Jing Dynasty in 326 A.D., premier Wang Taw offered Kou Hong a position as officer of state. It is a beginning position in government and not of high importance, yet Kou Hong would have had an opportunity to become promoted. Regardless, he excused himself from any position of higher honor. He did not enjoy the glamorous life.

At that time, in southeastern China, a rebellion was stirred up. The Emperor, Cheng Ti, ordered one of his generals, Governor Ku Bih, to lead an army to subdue the insurrection. Ku Bih was an old friend of Bao Shuan, and before he started for the southeast he went to visit Bao Shuan. Bao Shuan treated him to a dinner also attended by his son-in-law, Kou Hong, where General Ku Bih met Kou Hong. He immediately knew him to be a special person. He heard the depth of Kou Hong's understanding through his speech and asked Kou Hong's views about his mission: "Now, in the southeast, some bandits have begun to make a disturbance. There has been unrest, trouble and violence for a thousand square miles. I have been ordered to go conquer them, but I have not decided the best way to proceed. You seem quite knowledgeable. I would be interested in your advice on this matter."

Kou Hong replied, "I am an ordinary civilian who knows little about military strategy. However, the bandits are also civilians. I have heard about the rebellion, and the great restlessness of the people. Could it be that they are struggling against suffering that is caused by hunger and cold? I do not think the government has paid much attention to the living conditions there. The court has no sympathy for the people, and the government forces them to pay a tax so heavy that the people do not have enough left to live on. This is why they have become fearless and caused trouble. I do not think they have any real ambition or wish to compete with the throne. It is just a momentary trouble.

"It appears to me that military force will only make the trouble worse. I think peace can be attained in a different way; I wish you would have sympathy for these people and the conditions of their lives. It would be the blessing of both the people and the government if you would do so."

When General Ku Bih heard this, he agreed with Kou Hong and liked what he had heard. He told Bao Shuan, "Your son-in-law is not only a scholar, he also understands problems deeply. I think this suggestion is really beneficial. Will you give me permission to take your son-in-law with me? He can help me handle this problem." Kou Hong immediately refused, saying, "What I say is just conversation. I do not think I can really handle anything." Nevertheless, with this opportunity, Kou Hong began to play an important role in the military action of the government under General Ku Bih.

He proved to be invaluable in negotiations between the government and the hungry people and was thus instrumental in ending the trouble in the southeast. This gave him much credit in the eyes of the government, and he was rewarded by being made a duke. Nevertheless, Kou Hong hesitated to accept the title. It was not his original intention to have either a name or position. He was only interested in following the example of his great uncle: to achieve himself spiritually and to learn about immortal medicine.

In his studies, Kou Hong had learned of a substance called cinnabar that can assist an individual's immortal medicine by helping to pacify the internal spirits through other ways. The cinnabar produced in Kou Lou was said to be the best cinnabar. Kou Lou is the area which is now the border of Kwangton, Kwaysi and Viet Nam; during Kou

Hong's time this was still within Chinese territory. This place was still wild, so at first Kou Hong wished to excuse himself immediately from receiving the title and position, but then he thought that he would like to go to Kuo Lou to obtain some cinnabar for his refinery. He also had some interest in touring the countries of southern Asia. So he said, "Give me a lower position. I do not need to be a Duke. Perhaps I could be the magistrate of Kuo Lou, in the outskirts." That was not what the government had planned, but it was finally agreed upon, because at that time it was still quite a barbaric spot and somebody was needed to manage it. They still gave him the title of Duke, but allowed him to do only the work of a simple magistrate. Kou Hong was happy about this, and he and his wife collected their things and moved to Kuo Lou.

Kuo Lou was a small county. When Kou Hong took his position, he reduced taxes, stopped using people for free labor, stopped litigation among people and lightened the punishments for crimes. It took only several months to make this small place become peaceful, and then he did not have much to do.

Kou Hong and his wife lived near a special mountain called Loufu where he frequently went to visit. In his wish to study the meaning of life, he studied the mountain and noticed that in spring and summer the mountain was lush and green, while in fall and winter, the vegetation became dry and withered. Then he thought, nature has a cycle of prosperity and decline. What is the force that makes that happen?

He also saw that in the winter there is a time when the plum flowers blossom. Some flowers open up, but some fall to the ground. He understood a little about chi, and he thought, "Some flowers blossom and others fall because of the chi behind them. When the chi is strong, a flower opens; when the chi is weak, a blossom withers. All life depends upon chi. No one can live without inner chi. When life is young, people are strong, because chi is in them. When people become old, that chi starts to be exhausted. So people who wish to live long must always nurture their chi. They must always help the chi be strong, and not

weaken or exhaust it. This is why the *Book of Refining* &k
Immortal Medicine teaches each person to nurture chi."

From that moment on, every morning and evening Kou
Hong started practicing nurturing chi. He did it by practic- *Meditate*
ing sitting meditation. At the beginning, he just kept quiet.
Then, later, he learned to adjust his breathing. The following is what he learned: Exhale the old energy with a poofing
sound, then take in the new energy. Nurture the energy and *Breathing Method*
keep it in the tan tien. Once the energy is strong in the tan
tien, it will reach the tailbone. From the tailbone it will
move slowly upward through the spinal cord until it reaches
the top of the head.

By doing this, Kou Hong's internal energy became
stronger each day. His bodily functions were strong and he
felt happy. He wondered, "Where did this happiness come
from? It must come from inside, because nothing from
outside has come to me. Many people look for happiness
and reward from outside but they do not nurture themselves
to find lasting happiness. Now that I understand that what
is internal is more important than what is external, even
doing this job is not worth it." Kou Hong had already been
in Kuo Lou for three years, and now he asked leave, saying,
"I am sick, I cannot do this job any more."

So Kou Hong left the position and went back to his
home town. He saw his father-in-law and said, "Your son-
in-law has been doing a job for three years and has only
filled his sleeves with air." (Most government officials take
gold or other valuable things, but Kou Hong did not.)
"However," he continued, "I brought back a chest filled with
cinnabar to give to you. Perhaps you can make use of it as
one element to refine the external medicine." Bao Shuan
was happy to receive it. He said, "With this, I can turn base
metals into gold and silver, and I will not need to borrow
money from anyone."

From then on, the father-in-law and son-in-law did not
go out any more. They did the energy practices for the
internal medicine and worked together on the refinement of
base metals into gold, which is called external alchemy. It
took some months, but they finally achieved the ability to
use cheap metals to make gold and silver. Not only did they

have enough money to support their own lives without having to work for the government, but they also used some of the money to help people in need. Yet they knew very well that gold and silver bring no benefit to one's true life and that the true goal of material support was to provide the time to cultivate themselves, Their main interest was not to turn base metal into precious metal, but it became well known that they could do so. Later they knew that it was not real gold.

This part of the tradition has changed in modern times. We need to earn our financial support through our own labor. With that support, each individual refines his own immortal medicine without utilizing or relying on the method of external alchemy any more. A student asked, "Why is external alchemy no longer as useful as it once was?" My answer is because it was not real gold.

A Duke who was a descendant of Liu An, an achieved immortal of the Han Dynasty (206 B.C.- 219 A.D.) was still in favor with the government despite the fact that the dynasty had changed several times. This person's interest was the refining of external medicine or alchemy, but he had not yet received the secret. Here we are talking about changing base metal to gold. Many times he tried to do it without success, but he did not give up looking for a good teacher to help him.

When he heard about Kou Hong, he sent messengers with gifts and invitations. At first, Kou Hong refused to see him, but he eventually believed in the person's sincerity and went to meet him. The Duke was no longer a Duke, because his title was from a past dynasty, but he still had a strong background. He treated Kou Hong well and asked him to teach him the method of refinement. Kou Hong told him that although the refinement of personal energy depends on external means, personal success or failure in achieving immortal medicine really connects with natural mercy and the protection of the spiritual realm. Here they were talking about internal medicine, not external medicine. Kou Hong told the Duke, "If your highness wishes to help people in trouble, maybe you can succeed. The spiritual realm might help you so that your ordinary cheap metals may be successfully turned into gold and silver. If you only wish to enjoy personal wealth, I do not think the fruit of alchemy will satisfy you." The Duke said, "In this whole area, people owe the government tax. I would like to do this to help them pay the tax." In ancient times, the distinction between the ruler and the ruled was clear, and the ruled had to be taxed. There was no income tax system like we have today. At that time, it did not matter if you had income or not, or if the crops were plentiful or not, you had to be taxed if you were one of the ruled. If not, you were jailed or killed. At that time the whole area where he lived suffered from not being able to pay the tax. There was not much time before the punishment for failure to pay would begin.

Kou Hong agreed to help the Duke refine cheap metal into precious metal to help the people pay their taxes. This is a big thing he did for people.

However, Kou Hong thought, "I am doing precious metal alchemy almost every day, and I am busy for people, for external things. People thank me and spoil me with their gifts. How about my personal life, my true life? I must stay away from people and from my own family in order to find a suitable place to seek the truth and work on my achievement." Surely he did not have to worry about money because of his precious metals. So he changed his clothes to look like an ordinary person. He chose the name of Pau Po Tzu, took one assistant and went to find a new place to live. He did not live close to his family nor his hometown so that no one could trace him.

Kou Hong followed the Yang Tze river and went to Nan Jing. He kept traveling and went to Tanyang where Mother Chern once lived, and Souzhou, but he discovered that although those places were nice, they did not provide the protection he needed. They were not deep enough for hiding. He kept traveling until he reached Ling-An, which is now called Huangchow. There he saw the beauty of West Lake and its mountains. It was a special place under Heaven, so he was happy and said, "In this place I can live."

Kou Hong roamed all over looking for a suitable spot. He was not interested in the mountain of South Screen or Nan Ping mountain, which stuck out too much. He did not like the place called Ling Yin; it was too out of the way. He did not like the Mountain of Speculation because it was too shallow and exposed. He did not like the Stone House Mountain, it was too steep. One day, on the mountain of Perching Rosy Clouds, he saw a mountain to the west. Its ridge keeps turning and wriggling back and forth like a living dragon. To the South, he saw the Mountain That Swallows the Morning Sun. To the West, he could clearly see the moon shining at night, so he decided that it would be a good place to live and build a hut. There was a big stone on a spot where he could do meditation. There was good water, so it would be a place to set up a stove and cauldron for refining base metals. Having those tools came to be a symbol of being a certain type of person. Although people sometimes passed through the place, they would not stay there to enjoy the ruralness. Huangchow, a relatively close city, was a place with songs, music and fun, but it was quiet in this spot. After observing it, Kou Hong became happy and said, "This is my place." He took out some money produced in his special way, bought the land and built a small hut where he could live alone. He set up the stove and cauldron to turn more base metal into precious metal to support his spiritual purpose, and he settled there.

Every day he sat on the top of the mountain, observing the changes of nature, looking for the deep truth behind all changes. One day, he wrote a poem for himself:

> I allow my free mind
>   to search for the truth of life.
> My discovery is that nature, with the sky and earth,
>   is just a big stove.
> The energy is like white clouds soaring around.
> The fire comes from the red sun.
> Life needs to be continually refined.
> This is why one needs to continually
>   cultivate oneself.
>
> The spiritual womb for an energy baby can be successful
> After nine times of repeating this process and before ten.
> By refining your energy,
>   the holy baby will be born into the universe.

This was Kou Hong's understanding. He always wondered why nature never became old. It is because energy follows cycles. Humans who are born to a father and mother have a much shorter cycle than nature itself. Even if a person is young and strong, they soon become old and weak; human life does not last. Even if we do well and take advantage of natural energy by intaking it, at most it can only help a person add a few years. It can never help an already damaged body return to a perfect condition.

Kou Hong also thought, "If people could not achieve spiritual immortality, then the stories and teachings of immortals must be ridiculous. At least I know my great uncle whose achievement can be traced. His achievement was proof enough for me that it is not something ridiculous. From this, I believe that even if we are born into the world, there must be a way to return to the original being that existed before we were born.

"I have looked at the *Book of Refining Immortal Medicine*; the theory is delicate. It talks about internal fatherly and motherly energy, it talks about the yang earth and yin earth and about pregnancy and about attunement. It talks about giving birth to a baby boy and about the yang spirit's trip outside the body. The books and the immortals talk this way. I do not believe that they have falsely established a name to fool people.

"Those books also talk about a man of 3 and 7 and 9, and a woman of 2 and 6 and 8, the internal masculine and feminine energy. They talk about a match maker called the Yellow Lady. The people think this refers to a bed game of making love in the inner room. Yet, everybody has sex and I do not think sex makes most people become immortal. It must be a metaphor that people cannot understand. Although there is some practice or skill to sexuality, sex is something connected with the body, not with the high spirit. And also, as I have observed, if a man overly enjoys staying with affection from women, he is usually on the road to a fast weakening."

While Kou Hong had been magistrate of Kou Lou, he had done the practice of breathing and achieved some success by doing it every day. One day, he stayed in the

Terrace of the Sun Rising in that mountain, gently breathing in the morning energy from the East. He suddenly thought about a passage in the *Book of Refining Immortal Medicine*. It said, "If there are no true seeds in the stove, it is like using fire to cook an empty pot." Kou Hong thought again, "According to this passage, my way of breathing which takes the energy from nature is not of high value. The high value is the true seeds. What are the true seeds? They must be some kind of medicine. Also, the *Book of Refining Immortal Medicine* says that a worn-out bamboo basket can be repaired with bamboo. It also says that if you wish the eggs to hatch, you have to use the hen to hatch the eggs. However, I have observed that body energy all belongs to the category of After-Heaven. How can it be the true seeds?"

Sitting, lying down, and moving around, Kou Hong kept wondering, "What are the true seeds?" but he could not get the answer just by studying books.

One day, a spiritually achieved one who looked very old but healthy came to visit Kou Hong. He asked Kou Hong, "Do you have a place where I can stay overnight?" Kou Hong looked at him and saw that he had good energy, so he invited him in and asked him where he was from. The man told him, "I have come to tell you the true seeds." As soon as Kou Hong heard that, he bowed deeply and said, "Please, my teacher, tell me." The man stopped him from his deep bowing and said, "Brother, you do not need to be so polite, I am a student of your great uncle, Master Kou Shuan. I was told a long time ago to come and teach you what was passed down from him." So, this man taught him all the secrets of the important practices done by his great uncle.

Now Kou Hong suddenly lit up. This is what the immortal book talked about. The book said, "The young man of 3 and 7 and 9 is the father, and a girl of 2 and 6 and 8 is the mother. Both are internal energy. The yang earth and the yin earth is the harmony of the two types of energy; the Yellow Lady is the mind which conducts the intercourse between the two types of energy." This confirmed Kou Hong's understanding that this father and mother are not physical parents. The book was talking about fatherly and motherly internal energy. These two energies are yin and r *Pearl*

yang. The intercourse between those two energies produces a subtle pearl in the position between the eyebrows. This mystical pearl, therefore, is produced by the motherly yin energy and the fatherly yang energy that are both part of an *pearl* individual's own energy. Then, it is swallowing this pearl which creates the true seeds of the physical body. The true seeds are not what I call the particles of semi-spiritual energy.

Kou Hong understood that the intercourse between the father and mother was a battle. It takes time to produce the mystical pearl and it takes time to nurture it. It is the fruit of personal energy through refinement. If done correctly, the conception will succeed and when the time comes, an energy baby will be born. After the energy baby is born, the original spirits can live independently outside the body. (It is the decayable, mortal body which produces spirits.) After the birth of the spiritual energy baby, the exuviation will be true.

Now that Kou Hong had received Master Kou Shuan's instructions through the special visitor, Master Cheng Shih Yuan, he totally understood. Now there was no longer any puzzle or confusion. The old man left, and Kou Hong made some new plans. First, he took some money from where he had it hidden and gave it to his assistant to buy materials to build a new house. He wanted to change the house according to the energy arrangement of the natural surroundings, so that he could hide himself well without letting people know he was there. Originally, when living in a one-room hut, people could always tell when he was there, so he could always be found. Now, he made the house bigger, so it would still be enjoyable to stay there. People could not bother him.

The House #1

In the last section, there was a term mentioned that was used to describe the two internal energies. It was "a woman of 2 and 6 and 8 and a man of 3 and 7 and 9." Undeveloped people thought that those numbers in some way referred to their ages. Practically it is all metaphoric. The image of a woman, and the even numbers, two, six and eight, represent yin energy. The image of a man and the odd numbers, three, seven and nine, represent yang energy.

Each number represents a different stage of female and male energy.

Now let us discuss the true seeds. Even true seeds take time to grow. After some time of concentrated spiritual cultivation, you integrate the yin and yang energy within yourself. Then you feel something happening; although you cannot see it, hear it or touch it, you can feel the mystical pearls, one or more, shaping themselves in your head. Once it (or they) become shaped, it (or they) become stronger and stronger. That is not the final step. The true seed, or seeds, still must be nurtured and be brought down from the forehead through gentle conduction, into the deep trunk called the Yellow Court. The Yellow Court is a term that describes energy or a location of energy, not an organ. Undeveloped people say it is close to the navel, about one or two inches above it.

In the *Story of Two Kingdoms*, the Yellow Court is the heart area. It cannot be rigidly defined because it is a little different for different people. It is deep inside, practically. So at this step, now you have medicine, you have seeds.

In his new house, Master Kou Hong closed the door and did not make any trips or outings. He closed the drapes and did not even look out the windows. Every day he sat with the cauldron and the stove. Please understand that this is a metaphoric description; there is no house, no window, no cauldron and no stove in a material sense. It is all meant in an internal sense. Shutting the door and closing the drapes are also metaphors that mean shutting off the scatteredness of the mind. By internal exercise, the water in the cauldron above the stove is warmed up by the fire. That is a metaphor that means the sexual energy is vaporized and rises to the higher area of the head. Now, Kou Hong needed to wait for the appearance of the true seeds that were the spiritual essence or spirit before being born with a certain form of special energy. That is called True Seeds of Pre-Heaven.

Then the Yellow Lady of the Earth, the matchmaker, every day conducted the handsome gentleman expressed by the numbers 3 and 7 and 9 and the beautiful woman expressed by the numbers 2 and 6 and 8 to meet each other. They played with each other all the time in front of the cauldron and stove of Kou Hong. There were some disturbing thieves called dragons and tigers, but still, the male yang energy and the female yin energy harmonized and blended. By the way, in the alchemical texts, yin and yang are also respectively called lead and mercury. Each attracts the other without needing anything to force them. However, the attraction between the two depends upon the conducting of the Yellow Lady.

At a special moment, the golden boy and the jade girl, the refined yang and yin energy, in their spot between the eyes and the eyebrows showed a pearl of purple color. Kou Hong immediately opened the drape of the window to look at it. He now immediately knew that this was the seeds of pre-Heaven of the physical father and mother. He immediately began to breathe to add more fuel into the stove. The fire is the mind, but the mind has to be controlled and carefully protected. No negligence should happen.

After some time, inside the trunk or belly, something feels different. You know you have true seeds; you do not need any more immortal medicine. At this time, you cannot have any ambition or expectation about your practice. Your mind needs to be clean and clear. Otherwise it will lead to misconception. Keep your mind single-pointed upon the internal warmth, and keep it steady without impatience, laziness or carelessness. This is the true secret of cultivating Spiritual Essence, and it is the way to integrate physical reality with mystical reality. Inside of you, the true seeds are conceived. Every month will be different; it is just like a pregnant woman needs nine months of gestation for a child. It takes a different length of time for each person depending upon his or her situation. After that time passes, the fetus is mature and is born. You will feel similar to an ordinary woman giving birth to a mortal child, but it is born through the head instead of the reproductive organs, and you are giving birth to a child made of energy. It can travel far too. Then this child will become the true god within and without your being. Thus, when you have actualized your subtle body, you can do whatever you wish on the subtle sphere and live an unlimited life that no longer relates to

true
Jm

age, form and experiences, or just wait for the time you choose.

Kou Hong reached that point and his long years of ambition were fulfilled. His determination in cultivation of spiritual energy produced fruit. He was thankful to Heaven, earth and his ancestors, so he made a vow to practice medicine and help people, but do so in a way that he would not be attached to the world. He sent his assistant home to help his family understand that there was no hope of his returning to live an ordinary life. Every day, he was happily enjoying himself in the region near West Lake. He concealed his achievement in spiritual energy and his special psychic attainment and made no show of what he had achieved. Every day he went out of the house, and sometimes just stayed on the mountain peak. Sometimes, even though he was out for ten days or more, he did not feel the need to eat. In winter he did not feel cold, and sometimes rain could not make him wet. Fire could not burn him. His way of life made him different from other people. His old friends and acquaintances were astonished and admired him.

One day, a man who had social prestige or position invited him to have dinner with a gathering of many scholars or noble people. One person was teasing him in a challenging manner and said, "We heard your granduncle knew magic and that he could spit out the rice in his mouth and transform them into bees. I do not know if that is true or not." Kou Hong answered, "Rice is rice. Bees are bees. How can they be changed? That may or may not be true about my ancestor, I do not know, but I would like to follow your wish." So he opened his mouth. Originally he was chewing rice, but he blew out the rice into the man's face. The man thought it was rice and shook his head to keep it off him, but he suddenly noticed that it was a big swarm of bees attacking his face. The man used his big sleeves to drive the bees away, but the bees were coming from all directions and he could not stop them from stinging him. At this point, he yelled, "Please forgive me, now I know my fault." Kou Hong laughed, "This is rice, how can it sting you? Look, it is still rice." Kou Hong raised his chopsticks, and the big swarm of rice flew back into his mouth. This occasion made Kou Hong's name become more famous.

On another occasion, the magistrate of Tien Tan county was having a picnic at the harbor and invited Kou Hong to join them and see the tide. The tide of Tien Tang River was high, dangerous and strong, but beautiful to watch. I think it was shaped partly by underground rocks. Many people used the tide for a special occasion to gather friends or family together, so that official invited Kou Hong for dinner.

Before the dinner, the people were all enjoying wine together. During the wine drinking, suddenly the tide came in; it was strong like a mountain pushing forward. The people could see it; it looked like the snow wave of a silver mountain rushing toward them. But because all the people were so close to the harbor at the riverside, they all got up to run away because it was so strong. The person who invited Kou Hong stood up and wished to run, but Kou Hong would not let him. He kept him there, saying, "We have come here to watch the tide, now the tide is coming. If we run away, then we cannot see it, and then what is the purpose of coming here?" The man answered, "I would like to watch it, but I do not want it to carry me away." All the people rushed over to the high bank, and left Kou Hong sitting there alone. Kou Hong stayed there, enjoying his drink. In one critical second, the tide came so strong. Kou Hong raised his cup to the strong rushing wave in front of him, and suddenly the wave stopped and could not go further. Everybody on the top could see that the tide split and went on two sides so the place where Kou Hong sat had not one drop of water.

On another occasion, Kou Hong and a friend were on a boat in West Lake. They were discussing talismans. A talisman is a spiritual word written on a piece of paper which can determine or influence an event. The friend asked Kou Hong, "Is there any paper on the boat? I heard that talismans are effective, do you know how to use them?" Kou Hong said yes, and he took a piece of paper, wrote some words on it and then threw it into the water. The paper followed the flow of the wake from the boat. His friend said, "This is not anything special, because anybody can throw paper in the water and watch it float away." So Kou Hong took another piece of paper, wrote something on it and threw it over the side of the boat. Now the water was flowing in a different direction and the paper followed that flow. The guest said, "The water direction must have changed direction because of a gentle wind. That is nothing unusual." Kou Hong then wrote another talisman and threw it into the water. However, this time the water became perfectly still, and did not flow in any direction, right or left, front or back. The piece of paper stayed circling there, and the other two pieces of paper came and joined it. So the man on this occasion understood that if a person has power, his writing also has power.

Writing Power

On another occasion, Kou Hong took a walk along the broken bridge, a famous spot on West Lake. A fisherman caught a big fish but unfortunately the fish died. A live fish, you see, can be sold at a much better price, so the fisherman was unhappy about it. When Kou Hong met him, he said, "If you will sell this dead fish to me cheaply, I would like to buy it." "Okay," the man said, "you pay me and I will give it to you." So he sold him the fish. Kou Hong bought the dead fish and then wrote some words on a piece of paper. He put the paper in the mouth of the fish and put the fish in the water. The fish swam away. The fisherman exclaimed, "If I had known it was alive, I could have sold it for more money; what a pity to have sold it so cheaply."

Another time, Huangchow had a drought. People were all troubled because most of them made their living by farming at that time. Many religious people were praying for rain; this is Chinese custom, but it did not succeed. Rain did not come. Some of the people told Kou Hong about the drought. He said, "I will see how I can help you." The next day at sunrise, he went over to his well and drew out some water. He put the cup to his lips as though he was going to drink it, but after putting the water in his mouth, he blew it out, spraying it in all directions. In no time, great dark clouds had formed and at least ten inches of rain fell upon the land.

On another occasion, a poor fellow who used to work by carrying water to sell to people carelessly lost his money when his coins fell into the deep well. The man was unhappy and cried, saying, "All my hard work is gone to waste." Kou Hong said, "Foolish man, you do not need to cry, I will help you." He stood on the side of the well and yelled, "Money, come out." One after another, the coins flew out of the well, and not a single penny was lost. The man watched him in amazement and thanked him.

One year, there was a dangerous, contagious disease called cholera. Many people died from it. Kou Hong wrote some special words on a piece of paper and threw it into the well. He made the people drink the water, and all of them were cured.

Another day, a man who was forced to pay tax and did not have the money decided to sell his wife to pay the tax and avoid being jailed. The wife could not accept the bad situation, so she tried to kill herself so she would not be sold. "How can he sell me? It is against all dignity." Kou Hong saw her and stopped her, saying, "You do not need to do that; I will make it so that you can live a long happy life together with your husband. Somewhere there is a pine tree with a big stone underneath it. Under the stone, a bandit hid a parcel with some money. Ask your husband to go take it; it is not only enough to pay the tax, but you will also have enough to start a new business." When she sent her husband to the tree, the money was there, just as Kou Hong had said, and all went well for the couple's new business.

Another time, Kou Hong was the host at a large gathering of people. The gathering had begun and Kou Hong and the people were sitting at the table in the big hall. Some of the guests arrived late, but no matter what time they arrived, they said that they were all greeted at the door by Kou Hong. However, the people sitting at the hall said he never once got up out of his seat.

When people went to visit him at his house, some people remarked that his house was very cold. Kou Hong blew out a little air from his mouth, and the house became as warm as though there was a warm desert wind. In the summertime when they visited, they remarked that the house was very hot. So Kou Hong would blow out a little air from his mouth and the house became as cool as a mountain breeze.

Kou Hong was not fond of social engagements. Many people invited him and tried to persuade him to visit after he declined an invitation. Once people were begging him to attend a feast, but Kou Hong was reluctant. He told them, "I have a stomachache," and then he lay down on the ground and died. The man who invited him panicked and wanted to carry him to a doctor, so they picked up his arm to lift him, but the arm broke. They tried the other arm but it broke too. Everywhere they touched broke. Then, in one second, worms began to grow from the corpse. The distraught man rushed away to get his family to tell them what happened. To his surprise, when he entered his house, Master Kou Hong was quietly sitting in the living room. The man did not say anything and when he went back to look for the corpse, nothing was there.

By the time he was old, Kou Hong could no longer live undisturbed near West Lake, because everybody knew he was immortal and came to him looking for favors. Thus, he went back to his old home town. When he went back, his father-in-law and wife were no longer in the world. They had both achieved themselves as immortals. Kou Hong felt sorrow that they were no longer there, so he went to live with the descendants of his family. When he stayed with them, they wrote down the book called *Pau Po Tzu* and the other medicine book of information he taught them. These books are popular and helpful to Chinese society.

Because he did so many interesting things and made people know he was a special person, he did not really enjoy living in the world because of his authority. All people came to look for his help or something else. At the age of 81, he used to spend a lot of time in cultivation in his room, just sitting as if asleep, without talking or moving. One day, his relatives discovered he had already exuviated, but his color was still like an alive person and his body was still soft and warm. When they took the corpse to put it into the coffin, it was very light. These unusual things made them know that his life of cultivation was different from the life of an ordinary person.

After many generations, after many dynasties had come and gone, people continued to visit Kou Ridge of the mountain of Kou, which were both named in his memory. A suitable place can help a person's cultivation, so many people visit there just to commemorate him. There is nothing left on the mountain, just the name as a memory of a spiritual person who lived in the world and made a contribution. However, his spirit is immortal within the sincere students who pursue the subtle spiritual truth.

Parts of the original material of Kou Hong's story were passed around by the people in the area of Huangchow. Around the Ming Dynasty, 1,000 years after Kou Hong ascended, a scholar gathered all those pieces, including some writing by Kou Hong's relatives about his story. The story was written in an unorganized but original style. I have made only a few adjustments for accuracy. He is the first master of the subtle spiritual truth who wrote a responsible book, *Pau Po Tzu*, and gave some details. At the end of his book, he also wrote down his own autobiography. Why don't I directly choose to translate his autobiography, but instead give the story? Because the story is much easier to read. Still, there are a few things I would like to adopt from the autobiography to add to this story.

First, his participation in the war may seem unusual. I am referring to the time when he helped avoid a battle during the insurrection. In Chinese culture, Confucian scholars carry the ceremonial spirits of the ancient Chinese. The interests of a student of universal subtle truth are more versatile; they include all aspects of life. Interestingly enough, war is a subject of their study, with two main principles: 1) Win a war through no war. 2) If there is no alternative to war, when fighting, reduce the killing to as little as possible by applying strategy. Thus, Kou Hong studied ancient military arts and did not hesitate to help improve the situation. In present day China, the communist party accuses Kou Hong of suppressing the farmers' liberation. They do not mention or see the truth. Through applying good strategy, Kou Hong reduced the killing and taught the leaders to make military action be effective.

The second thing this story did not describe was that at that time, Chinese martial arts were already developed as specific artistic achievements. Kou Hong himself was a student of martial arts with excellent achievement. That gave him confidence in life.

Kou Hong also traveled widely for the purpose of gathering medicinal material. Such traveling was seldom seen among ancient people. He traveled outside of China to almost all the countries of the Asian continent and also visited many cities within China.

We can attribute the passing down of his collection of ancient spiritual books to Master Kou Hong. These books contained spiritual practices from before written history of the time of Three Emperors: Heaven, Earth and People. The practices are effective, and I consider the books to be trustworthy. My personal interest is not in the teaching that arose after the Taoist religion formed but rather in the material that was written before folk Taoism and all its different sects. The ancient materials carry the essence of the subtle spiritual truth. They were not written for social promotion.

When I was young, I had a chance to come in contact with the collection Kou Hong made. Because he taught immortality, unless I met him, such teaching would not be trusted by me. I decided I would like to meet Master Kou Hong spiritually. In the spiritual realm, an immortal, natural spiritual deity or a spirit can be requested to visit or summoned. At that time, I took a book from my father's library that dealt with the practice of the Thunder School. I really did not know if it was the right way to establish communication with an immortal. I used the magic spiritual words sort of like a written talisman or as an order from an ancient king to his generals. I sent five knights to bring Master Kou Hong to meet me, an undeveloped boy. I was quite young and did not know that summoning immortals was not as simple as what I tried to do, but I went to sleep with the expectation that Master Kou Hong would come to meet me. At midnight, I dreamt that the five generals came with a rope to catch me and bind me up, and I came to my senses as if it had been a real thing. I had two reactions from my deep heart. 1) I had used the wrong method. (I had used the spiritual practice for subduing demons to apply to a master.) 2) I thought I was Master Kou Hong, or at least, some part of my spiritual element or personal tendency. However, I could not prove this identification. I do not insist it is true. This could have been a spiritual experience of my rough or modern attitudes before I became more involved in the exploration of the spiritual world.

Master Kou Hong did not become directly involved in building a worldly religion called Taoism, but his spiritual influence still reaches far and wide. In particular, Kou Hong directly and indirectly influenced the establishment of the San Ching School of Mao Mountain, which originated several generations after he lived. Its fourth Master, Taoh Hong Ching, wrote 20 volumes to explain the *Pau Po Tzu.* Without that explanation, the description of the internal practices of the *Pau Po Tzu* could not be understood. The book called *Pau Po Tzu* still exists, but unfortunately the good work of Master Taoh Hong Ching was lost.

In the autobiography of Kou Hong, no mention was made of magic, so the *Pau Po Tzu* is now appreciated by a few special individuals. It cannot be fully understood unless a person has natural inspiration and has restored part of his spiritual capability to be able to see and know the secrets of this book.

The story of Kou Hong illustrates that natural spiritual truth can be learned by most people. For someone who is learning the Integral Way, he is a bridge to the immortal world.

Master Kou Hong also cultivated himself on the Lotus Flower Peak of Tien Tai Mountain of Chekiang province. That peak was called the Lotus Flower Peak because the peaks surrounding it were like petals circling and embracing the center of a flower. Master Kou Hong's direct students lived in Huangchow and in Tien Tai Mountain. Because he did not formalize his teaching into a religious shape, the teaching of Master Kou Hong was passed down from individual to individual for generations.

Master Kou Hong's important practice is alchemy. Alchemy in ancient times was also called "refining the medicine." Basically, it took minerals and used a certain process to produce a medicinal product to support health. The original purpose was to use the medicinal product for immortality.

The discovery that certain medicine could be used to achieve immortality had several effects. The first came from the knowledge of the ancient, spiritually achieved ones. They knew that a person's life is energy. When the essential energy is scattered, then one's spirits scatter and one dies. How can the individual spirits still remain cohesive as one piece of energy, as an individual spiritual being? One way is to use refined minerals. If you go methodically, step by step, and your mind is not full of activity like ordinary people, the mental spirits will slowly converge and become unified. All the spiritual functions of the body, in fact, become one. Thus, the so-called immortal medicine (the spirits) can exist with or without the physical body.

Another way is one that the ancients discovered: human people carry certain germs that are harmful to life. The product from the refinement of minerals can also control or disable harmful germs or cure certain parts of the physical body. This development can only be utilized by a truly achieved master. Let me explain why. During the Han Dynasty, many scholars tried to use a medicinal powder made of five minerals. Some suffered greatly from their misguided attempts. It was a preliminary stage of science to know that human life needs the support of some mineral elements, but unfortunately those scholars did not know their correct use, so the practice of immortality was greatly blamed for the misuse of medicines.

In the *Pau Po Tzu*, Kou Hong talked a lot about these things. He learned from his teacher, Cheng Shih Yuan, who learned from his great uncle, Kou Shuan. Kou Shuan learned from Tzo Tsu. None of them were harmed by the mineral medicine produced by refinement using a certain practice. Using refined minerals is the emphasis of his teaching.

After many generations, several Tang Dynasty emperors died from taking the immortal medicine because they used their immortal medicine for the wrong reasons. They used

Set

it to support their sexual energy. It was never the purpose of the immortal medicine to support anyone's sexual activity. This was a different practice of later generations. Because the practice was written metaphorically and not clearly stated in the books, I suppose that it is inevitable that such a good thing would become misused. It was a free society at that time, and of course many people arose who claimed they were authorities on the subject when actually they knew nothing. Thus people died by using the medicine. Nobody was there to tell what mistakes needed to be avoided and so forth.

From the teaching of Kou Hong, one important lesson can be learned: the true teaching of natural spiritual truth is not a dogmatic belief or faith. Why? Because realizers of the natural spiritual truth of life emphasize the refinement of the medicine. They value the good, step-by-step change of raw material into high material. They take something useless and make it useful. Although there was uncertainty, the correct process and correct practice brought about success. The student who learns the natural subtle truth should heed this important principle: you do not learn the Integral Way as a ready concept or a formula to fit all situations. You learn principles and apply them to different situations correctly, so that you can be useful and helpful.

The practice of refining immortal medicine has become part of Chinese medicine, but if it is to be of any use, students still need to learn its real purpose and training. As I described, and as the *Pau Po Tzu* described, you can also achieve immortality in a different way, but Kou Hong never killed or harmed anyone by refining minerals such as gold, cinnabar or mercury. It was unachieved ones or impostors who made trouble. People who lack full achievement or knowledge still claim authority about those things. This type of thing happens in the world, but the pure practice or the pure achievement of the natural subtle truth and respectable leaders and qualified teachers of long ago should not be blamed.

Chapter 2

Kou Hong:
A Man of Embracing Spiritual Essence

Master Kou Hong was an important teacher for the later developed religious Taoism, yet his own life and activity were beyond the formality of a religion. I consider him more of a spiritual model than a common religious leader, so his life has to be clearly studied.

The first story of Kou Hong's life came from the people of Huangchow who admired him greatly. Now I would like to give you a more serious biography of his life, which has been gathered from the records of Chinese history. I hope that these two different and true versions of his life give my readers a more accurate impression of Master Kou Hong. Because his spiritual influence is wide and deep, the later religious Taoism used his foundation. This historical record tells about the unadorned part of his life. Some of it repeats what was said in the first version of Kou Hong's life.

According to the records of the Jing Dynasty, Kou Hong was born in 283 A.D. and ascended in the year 363, thus he enjoyed 81 years. Most scholars accept these dates. His ancestors and family were mostly farmers, and were not active in politics. Of course, the ancient type of politics was not similar to the modern type of politics; back then political positions were just social positions. His great uncle, however, was a true achiever of natural spiritual truth who had learned from Master Tso Tzu. This great uncle, Kou Shuan, cultivated himself in several mountains and had over 500 students. One of his achieved students was Master Cheng Shih Yuan, who was also called Cheng Yein.

Kou Hong was the third son in his family. He was much loved by his parents. His parents did not push him to study but he had a natural interest for it. At age 13, his father passed away. Then the life source was gone, so Kou Hong was forced to work in the fields, and he became a farmer. He used the time between the busy working hours to study. Unfortunately, war occurred, and all the books in the family library were burned. Nevertheless, Kou Hong did not give up his interest in study. He would walk a long way to borrow books from other families who still had books and bring them home to study. He was determined and studied widely. He did not have money for paper and calligraphy brushes, so he cut firewood to sell so that he could buy them. If he felt a book was good or useful, then he would copy and recite it.

At the age of 15, Kou Hong started to write poetry and articles. At age 16, he started to study some of the Chinese classics. Since he could not totally understand the ancient language in which they were written, he went to one of the achieved students of his great uncle, Ching Su Yuan (who was also called Cheng Yein), and asked him to be his teacher.

Master Cheng Shih Yuan was originally a great scholar. He knew all the classics well and also the principles and systems of the Chinese calendar. In his old age, he devoted himself to learning the natural spiritual truth and studied with Master Kou Shuan, the uncle of Kou Hong. Master Cheng Shih Yuan received the ancient books of practicing the natural spiritual practice from Kou Shuan and studied all of them one by one. Although he achieved mastery in what he learned, he used the traditional Confucian classics to teach his students, who respected him.

During the period he learned from Master Cheng Shih Yuan, Kou Hong did not concentrate on one thing. He explored many things, looking to understand things that were not clear to him yet. In this period, he finished reading or copying ten thousand books. Those books were more for training or only to use for quotations when he wrote; they did not make him a scholar or a teacher of scholars. His wide reading included all the good books passed down from the ancients, the pictures, the arts, mathematics and the ancient system of foreknowledge. Later he learned some practices. He learned almost all of them. He also learned archery and how to use shield and weapons, achieving himself quite well in the martial arts. He also learned how to lead an army, engage in war, military strategy and so forth.

At this time, Kou Hong wished to write a book about his achievement so that in the future people could benefit from his contribution. At the same time, he nurtured the thought of choosing the life path of a civilian. He did not wish to be put in a political position. He respected and admired the ancient hermits or achieved civilians who did not possess social position.

Master Cheng Shih Yuan had over fifty students who helped him do agriculture, and at the side, studied and learned from him. I would like to explain a little bit about the ancient schools. You could call them student or spiritual communities. There was a teacher and students. At that time the land was free; a person only needed to put labor into developing it. No one fought for land, because there was so much available to use. There was no registration of ownership, either. People and society recognized that whoever put the energy into working the land owned the land and the crops.

Usually the teacher served the students simply by teaching, whereas students who were serious about learning from the teacher did the tilling and farming to provide whatever the teacher needed. The teacher was like a kind of governor, landlord or leader, but he was not the manager. Management was done by the elder or senior students, so there was no pressure of life. Mostly the management and real labor work was all done by the students. Lao Tzu and several of his students were teachers of this kind who headed a spiritual community.

Master Cheng Shih Yuan's library was rich and abundant. Master Kou Hong was not a physically strong type of person, and because he was the great nephew of Master Kou Shuan, Master Cheng Shih Yuan treated him a little differently than the others. He made Kou Hong work at copying the good books. Ancient books would often decay after about seven years, so they needed to be copied or preserved frequently. This provided Kou Hong with a special opportunity to come in contact with great ancient works the other students never saw.

Master Cheng Shih Yuan did not neglect to study the character of Kou Hong by closely observing him. After years of testing, he knew Kou Hong to be a trustworthy person and a good student, so he made the offering to Heaven in the Mountain of Horse Trace. He transmitted secret passages he had learned about golden medicine and high spiritual practices to Kou Hong, and also gave him some important books about the practice of the natural spiritual truth. Cheng Yein made these arrangements even though Kou Hong was not yet ready to learn the high secrets and know the spiritual mission he was to continue. Kou Hong still expressed scatteredness in some ways because his worldly interest was not finished, so Master Cheng Shih Yuan could not go into depth with him.

Around 302 A.D., Master Cheng Shih Yuan foresaw or understood that there would be military trouble in the form of a rebellion south of the Yang Tze river, so he led his students to hide themselves or become hermits in Ho mountain. Kou Hong did not go with the teacher, however. Kou Hong's study or scope of reading had become wider, and he now understood that he had not studied or achieved enough. He abandoned most of his old writings, keeping only about a tenth of them.

In 303 A.D., the rebellion started. A rebel army attacked Huangchow and Kou Hong began to worry whether his home town would be safe in this uprising of ambitious army officers. At that time, military riots were caused mainly by those who were looking for opportunity and military adventure. They were started by those who wished to compete for rulership and become the new emperor. Occasionally civilians rose up during times of difficulty, such as when there was a bad year and the crops were insufficient to provide for people's needs. Then some ambitious leader would start a riot. If the military uprising succeeded, no change really happened, because the old emperor was only replaced by a new emperor. Everything stayed pretty much the same. Then sometime later, another new military adventure would start and another new leader would replace the old. Because the social or political system did not change, common people suffered no matter who was emperor. Modern scholars think that the farmers had a reason for their uprisings, but nothing was actually changed or accomplished by the revolts. Changing systems is more important than changing leaders within the same system of monarchy.

Kou Hong received the summons of the general and went to his home town accompanied by several hundred young people who all joined in defending the safety of the home town. In this war, by his merit and achievement, Kou Hong officially became a general.

In 304 A.D., the trouble was over. Kou Hong also gave up the position of general, and set out on a trip. He headed toward the capital, Lou Yang, to search for good books. However, in 305 A.D. when Kou Hong was traveling there, he ran into trouble. The Rebellion of the Eight Princes, another military uprising, began and he could not go further toward the capital, nor could he turn back home, because behind him was another military uprising. Instead, he traveled widely, visiting different provinces.

In 306 A.D., a general was assigned to be governor of Huangchow. It was a wide region that covered the whole province now. This governor was an old friend of Kou Hong and had once made Kou Hong a military advisor. Instead, Kou Hong wished to go south to avoid the military riots in the north. Because the governor was his friend, he agreed to help him, so he went to Huangchow. Unfortunately, his friend the governor was killed by enemies, but Kou Hong stayed there and started writing his most important book, *Pau Po Tzu.*

Master Kou Hong stayed many years in Huangchow. At that time, it was not a developed city like it is today but was still quite rural. Because he had no interest in any social or political position, he stayed in Loufu mountain. It was at this time he made friends with Governor Bao Shuan, the governor of the Southern Sea (that is, the land and the people of the coastal region of the south, now still part of Kwang Tung). Bao Shuan was a true realizer of the natural truth and also had some foreknowledge about how the world was changing. He had learned from Masters Yin Ch'ang Seng and Tso Tzu. Governor Bao Shuan valued Kou Hong, so in 312, he gave him an important spiritual practice. Bao's collection was the earliest spiritual practice from an epoch called the Time of the Three Emperors as Heaven, Earth and People. After Kou Hong taught it to some students, this particular material became a special school of ancient spiritual practice. Bao Shuan also married his only daughter, Lady Bao Kou, to Kou Hong.

During this time, Kou Hong concentrated on cultivating himself, arranging his special diet and nurturing his spirit. He also continued to write the *Pau Po Tzu.*

In the year 314, Kou Hong and his father-in-law, Governor Bao Shuan, left the south and went back north to their home town of Tanyan in Jing Ling. At this time, Kou Hong went with the magistrate of You Hong, Gu Hien, to look for a great hermit, Ku Wen, who lived in the mountains of Ta Bi. After he came home, he was appointed local governor, a general's position, but he did not accept. He did not accept any other positions he was offered.

In 315 A.D., one of the princes become prime minister and was looking for talented people to help him. People recommended Kou Hong, but another military riot happened in 317 and the new emperor surrendered to the current force. The prime minister himself continued the emperor position in the new capital of the South. He choose one hundred and six capable ministers to help in the administration of the new government. Kou Hong was one of the ones chosen. It was during this year that Master Kou Hong accomplished the writing of the *Pau Po Tzu.*

In 317, the new emperor Yuan Ti (317-322) was enthroned. Because of Kou Hong's merit in having pacified the riot in his hometown many years earlier, the new emperor made him a duke, which gave him the privilege of accepting taxes from 200 families. Although Kou Hong strongly refused, his refusal was not accepted by the government. Finally, he accepted.

The capital moved from West to East during the Jing Dynasty. Under the Jing government in the East, too many changes happened and conflicts between the big scholastic families of north and south became stronger. The emperor gave some of them important positions, but the scholarly families of the south mostly gave up their positions and became civilians. They used the word "hermit" to describe someone who was not in a governmental position. In Western culture, a hermit is a person who totally stays away from people, but in China, hermit is someone who could have a high governmental position but prefers to live the life of an ordinary person.

Master Kou Hong had became a hermit in 322. But that year, one of the powerful ministers started a new rebellion. Most people who were in the royal court of Yang Ti were killed, thus he could not enjoy the peace of a hermit. That same year, Emperor Yang Ti died in the eleventh month.

One year earlier, in 321, as a hermit, Master Kou Hong wrote a poem about a new reservoir built by a local governor to praise the good work. This was his only public activity during this period of time. He stayed in the mountains for his spiritual cultivation until the year 326.

After some years of poor harvest, Master Kou Hong was summoned by the new regime to take a secondary position in the local government. Then he received a promotion. In the year 328, a new rebellion arose. Many cities were lost as the war was vigorously waged. Master Kou Hong again moved into the position of military adviser. At this time, the previously mentioned hermit Ku Wen died of an epidemic disease. His foreknowledge about the new military riot had been correct. Kou Hong respected Ku Wen greatly, so he and another of his friends worked together to write the biography of Ku Wen to exalt his firm character in times of confusion without sacrificing his personal spiritual dignity for worldly position.

The death of his friend refreshed Kou Hong's understanding of the inconstancy of mortal life and he returned to civilian life again in order to cultivate himself. He had been on several mountains of Chekiang province. He guided his students and nephews to experiment with external medicine. However, his friend Kang Bao thought that Master Kou Hong could help write the history of the government at that time, and he recommended Kou Hong for that position. Kou Hong had no interest whatsoever in doing so. By 333 Kou Hong had become older, and knew that he must refine his medicine for self-protection. He heard that cinnabar could be found in Kou Lou County, so he asked to become magistrate there. The emperor thought he was too noble for such a position and did not approve of making him a small magistrate, but Kou Hong insisted, saying, "I do not look for glory, but only for something to help me." The emperor finally agreed to his request and Kou Hong took his students and family to Kou Lou. I believe that Master Kou Hong simply had no interest in living in the midst of society.

The governor of Kuangchow kept Kou Hong there out of great concern; he did not let Kou Hong go to Kou Lou because it was still very a rough and barbaric place. He stayed on Loufu mountain again. However, the governor recommended to the emperor that he divide the big southern territory into two parts so that Kou Hong could administer one of the halves. The emperor approved the establishment of a new state, but Kou Hong insisted that he did not want to take the position. The governor of Huangchow made one of Kou Hong's nephews secretary of military affairs and this helped the situation, because if one person in a family was in the government, the whole family would be supported, thus Kou Hong did not have to worry about provisions. Kou Hong himself lived on Loufu mountain with his students and his other nephew, doing spiritual cultivation to refine the immortal medicine and writing books about natural spiritual truth.

In 344, on the third day of the third month in the Chinese calendar, Kou Hong gave the collection of spiritual treasure he had received from Master Cheng Shih Yuan to two of his nephews, Kou Wahng and Kou Shih, because they were also his students. Before Kou Hong ascended he sent a message to the governor, saying, "I shall go on a far trip to look for my teacher; I will start immediately." When the governor received this message, he immediately went to see Kou Hong. When he arrived, he found Kou Hong sitting in meditation as peacefully as though he were asleep; he had already ascended at noon. Even though he had already ascended, his body still looked alive. Most people think it is one proof of his achievement.

This part of his life was recorded by the official scholars. Now I am going to sum up the example he has given us. First, he embraced the simple essence of life. He did not pursue social fashion or float along with the changes of the world, looking for advantage. Second, he upheld the principle of self-contentment and satisfaction with what he could achieve. He did not look for anything other than what he won by his own merit. This was his life principle. Third, he preferred a civilian life, thus his values were different from those of other scholars who sought to elevate themselves with social glory. Unlike the other scholars, he did not study in order to pursue a governmental position, sharing the power of ruling over other people. He studied for his own understanding and benefit. He preferred civilian life to government work. He wrote down what he achieved and gathered from his wide studies. What he valued in life was different from the ordinary.

Fourth, he followed the typical spiritual attitude of helping the world politically through discussion. All true realizers of natural truth felt that everyone should share in political responsibility but not necessarily extend any political ambition. There is a difference between political responsibility and political ambition. Kou Hong talked about how to help the world. He wished to help the world, not extend himself to it. The leaders of the military rebellions competed for the throne and wished to manage the government as leaders of the world. There was no real value to that, because the system of monarchy or dictators did not change. What gives them the right to decide the laws, create regulations and practice control over the farmers or scholars? All changes in government were a waste, because even strong leaders had their decline.

Fifth, the example of Kou Hong's life is that he did not worship society and adhere to convention. He liked to face the problems of his day and accommodate the changes. This is the way of progress. In Chinese society when scholars support new leaders they usually use the psychology of yesterday to support the system of today. They think that the old systems, the old customs, the old way which helped the society of yesterday will work for today's problem, so they do not look for any changes. They cannot see the new generation and bigger population has new and different problems.

There is not just one tribe living in China, there are many, and as these tribes became stronger, they competed for leadership in the center of the big land. Finally, no peaceful society was achieved by anyone. Master Kou Hong differed from other scholars by pointing out that they realistically needed to look for a new direction.

Sixth, although he was a scholar, he made the goal of life to learn natural spiritual truth, and did not use his scholastic activities as a tool to obtain a position in government. Studying was to learn natural spiritual truth. He choose this as the final destination of his life.

We have heard a lot about Kou Hong, but there is one story that still exists in the library of biographies of spiritually achieved ones. Among the biographies of spiritual shiens, there were a few lines about the wife of Kou Hong. No one said much about her, but I would like to give this story about Kou Hong's wife, who was the daughter of Governor Bao Shuan. From the time she was very young, she liked to search for the subtle sphere. She stayed deep in meditation, not just sitting there; she just kept thinking deeply, contemplating life and the spiritual world. No one understood what she was doing, or what she was thinking.

Not long after her marriage, she died suddenly. Her face looked like she was still alive, so her father buried her in the mountains of Loufu. This was the mountain where Kou Hong went later to cultivate himself until the day he ascended.

Many years later, many generations later, a man called Tsui Wei went one day to Huangchow city, to visit a temple for prayer. On the way there, he saw a wine seller at the side of the road. An old lady had carelessly broken one of his wine jars. At that time, wine was carried in large jars. The owner was mad and was trying to beat the old lady. The young man, Tsui Wei, saw this and went over to interfere. He asked the man, "How much is your wine worth?" Then the owner told him how much it was worth, and Tsui Wei paid for it. The young man took off his beautiful overcoat, saying "I will have to use these clothes for money, because I walked out of the house without any cash. I will give you this coat as compensation for the old lady." The old lady did not even thank him, she just left. The next day, the young man met her again on the street. The old lady said, "Yesterday you helped me, so today I am going to help you. I have a special way to help you." She continued, "I do not have any way to pay you, but I can teach you something. I will teach you how to cure people's goiter by using moxibustion. This moxa is not the regular kind. It is a special herb I gathered." After passing that message and giving the herb to the man, she left.

Much later, the young man found an opportunity to use what she taught him. Somebody had a big goiter behind the ear, and when he used her method, the person was immediately cured. It was a monk that he cured. Shortly afterward, the monk took someone from a large, wealthy family who had a goiter to him for a cure. He was successful, and the news spread. He became famous; many people sought his help and he became rich. Nevertheless, he could not forget her, so he went searching for her. One day, someone told him that she was the daughter of Governor Bao Shuan, the wife of Kou Hong, and that she was still cultivating herself somewhere in the mountains. That is the only story left about this wonderful mystical lady.

This story describes the real Kou Hong. I have given you the true image of Master Kou Hong. His life and teaching is different from that of people who say they are Taoist teachers, but only make use of other people's fanciful thinking. Most who claim to be Taoist teachers are impostors. In truth, the Integral Way is so simple. You can learn the Integral Way from the *Tao Teh Ching*, the book of Chuang Tzu, or the later generation of truly achieved Zahn (Zen or Chan) masters. We do not talk about the religious form, but about the real practice of spirit. They continue the truthful natural spirit of being attached to nothing. They do not cheat people and live an almost ascetic type of life. That is a real example of the realization of the natural truth in life.

Another thing is that when people claim to have special powers, they often will use your psychological fantasy to cause you to lose money. A woman will lose her body for that kind of fantasy, so be careful. I myself have put a lot of energy into continuing the true teaching of the Integral Way from the ancient times. During the last few million years, people have had various spiritual or religious experiences. Many have found the truth. Usually whenever something is exalted, I feel it is my spiritual responsibility to tell you if it is real or not. A true realizer of the Integral Way does not really enjoy or feel proud of magic powers. What is important is the power of virtue. What is the difference between magic power and virtue power? With magic power, a person can use another person psychologically; in one moment the person will feel fantastic and become controlled by the first. Virtue, on the other hand, does not establish any control other than the person's own discipline. The value is in the person's character. It takes a long time to trust that person, but he does not work at you to make you trust him. He is just faithful in fulfilling his life. That is called the power of virtue. We follow the orderly and harmonious spirits. That is the normalcy of life, and that is a power.

Chapter 3

Instruction for Good Meditation

The Intercourse of Mind and Body: An ancient instruction for basic spiritual cultivation (Ryh Yong Ching). An ancient spiritual esoteric classic.

1) This discussion is about what should be done in a day of retreat, when eating and drinking has been fulfilled in a simple way and small amount. After taking a gentle walk, let one sit straight with his mouth shut and not allow a single thought to arise in his mind. Let him forget everything and keep his spirit quiet with settled purpose. Let his lips be glued together and his teeth be firmly pressed against one another. Let him not look at anything with his eyes, nor listen to a single sound with his ears. Let him watch over his inward feelings with all his mind. Let him inhale long breaths and gradually and slowly exhale. He should breathe in this way. It should be done without a break, now seeming to breathe and then not. In this way any excitement of the mind will naturally disappear, the water from the kidneys will rise up, saliva will be produced in the mouth, and the real benefit becomes effective to the life. It is thus that one acquires the way of prolonging life.

2) During the twelve hours of the day let one's thoughts be constantly fixed on absolute Purity. Where no contrary thoughts arise, we have what we call Purity. Where nothing of a contrary kind enters the Tower of Intelligence (the mind) we have what we call the Undefiled. The body is the house of the breath; the mind is the lodging of the spirit. As the thoughts move, the spirits moves; as the spirit moves, the breath is distributed. As the thoughts rest, the spirit rests; when the spirit rests, the breath is collected.

3) The true powers of the five elements unite and form the boat-like cup of jade, after partaking of which the body seems to be full of delicious harmony. This spreads like the balm of a thousand fragrant flowers on the head. Walking,

resting, sitting, sleeping, one feels one's body as flexible as the wind and in one's belly a sound like that of thunder. One's ears hear the songs of the Immortals that need no aid from any instrument; vocal without words and resounding without the drum. The spirit and the breath unite, and the bloom of childhood returns. The man beholds scenes unfolded within him; spirits of themselves speak to him; he sees things of empty mindedness and finds himself dwelling with the Immortals. He succeeds in making the Great Immortal Medicine and his spirit goes in and out of his body at its pleasure. The longevity of one's spirit equals that of Heaven and earth, its brightness that of the sun and moon. He has escaped the toils of life and death.

4) Do not allow any relaxation of your efforts. During all the hours of the day, strive always to be pure and undefiled. The spirit is the child of the breath; the breath is the mother of the spirit.

Just as a hen watches over and embraces its eggs, so can you preserve the spirit and nourish the breath. Can you do this without interruption? If you can, it is wonderful! The mystery becomes still deeper!

5) In the body there are seven precious organs which serve to enrich the state and give rest to the people. This metaphorically refers to one's internal system, which makes the vital force of the system full to overflowing. Hence we have the heart, kidneys, breath, blood, brains, semen (eggs) and marrow. These are the seven precious organs. They are not dispersed when the body returns to the dust if they have been refined by the use of the Great Medicine. They are the myriad spirits of body and all ascend among the Immortals.

This instruction should be applied to your meditation.

Visitor: I have continued a meditation which I learned from a different teacher. Now I would like to receive your instruction in order to help me attain its benefit.

Master Ni: Spiritual cultivation includes both sitting
meditation and movement. Both are deeply related and help
each other and should be practiced interchangeably. The
simplest way to meditate is by sitting. The knowledge and
skill of singular, sitting meditation can be applied to one's
physical exercise.   I recommend that people learn and
practice gentle physical movement. Taoist gentle physical
movement produces energy, chi. This is why all these
exercises belong to the category of Chi Kung (Chi Gong)
practice.

I welcome the discussion of your question from the
experience of simple meditation. However, quiet sitting is
not absolutely motionless, because there is still subtle
movement happening. When the beginner's mind learns to
regulate itself with the same principle exemplified by
external movement, this will lead to achievement.

*Q: Is the point of meditation to be totally present, or is it like
being concentrated? Sometimes if I am sitting, after I sit for
a while, everything kind of settles down and the experience
I have is that the energy in my head becomes clear. No more
thoughts happen. I think that is what meditation is about,
but I am not able to do that for long. Am I on the right track?*

Master Ni: You mentioned your personal experience. There
are two kinds of energy. If the impure energy stays on the
head, then your thoughts are not clear, and your vision is
not clear. Once the impure energy sinks down and the pure
energy rises to your head, you feel light. You feel your
vision is crystal clear, you feel light and happy, you feel joy.
This is experienced by many people. Impure energy means
to be fiery or with fast or abnormal blood circulation.

About the method of cultivation, sometimes I call it
complete concentration because it is easy for you to understand. When you do such a meditation, you should avoid
tightness. If your concentration is too tight, it will not help,
because the energy will not be flowing normally. When you
do meditation, let all systems and organs relax. Let the
internal functions, such as circulation, secretion and all
other systems come to their high efficiency in doing their

work. This is natural. It is not abiding the commands of your head, your mind.

It is important to stop the commands from the head. We continuously build a habit of using our mind. We wish to use our mind to make something happen a certain way, but the internal body functions are totally natural. Stopping the disturbing thoughts, stopping the commands from your mind, letting the body take care of the body, and letting the function help the function itself without any interference from the mind is the basic requirement for meditation. This also expresses the principle of wu wei, non-doing.

Also in meditation, if someone is too serious or focuses on thoughts or a suggestion, the result will not be natural. So before entering meditation, all suggestions should be avoided. When you enter meditation, there are some requirements, like being internally clean (i.e., not needing to go to the bathroom) and externally clean. Then sit in a suitable environment and prevent any possible disturbance. Maintain good relaxation and concentration.

There are many other purposes of meditation or quiet sitting. There are also many practices that can help a person achieve something, like sharpening one's vision, opening the Heavenly Eye or gathering one's energy to be ready to give birth to a red or immortal baby and so forth. What you are talking about is general meditation as a preparation for a specific cultivation. What you mentioned is a good habit to have, or a general common practice, but it cannot be said to be what meditation is all about.

I can confirm one thing. Many people wish to do something in meditation, and so they learn some practice. People have been organized this way by certain spiritual groups. The way of having an unnatural command is not better than wu wei, which is letting the body take care of itself, letting the mind take care of itself and letting the spirit take care of itself, everything going smoothly and beautifully.

Q: If a person gets up and sits in meditation every day, and they are not supposed to see anything, and they are not supposed to feel anything (you mentioned that feeling heat

*was still semi-physical), then what is supposed to happen?
I think a lot of people try to meditate for years and years and
they do not know what is supposed to happen or how to tell
if they are doing it right.*

Master Ni: There are several different meditation programs
and different methods of teaching. Basically, I still think
that just to sit quietly and calmly and not be in a gloomy
mood will be beneficial to any person. It maintains one's
emotional, psychological and physical health. However, it is
a terrible thing for a person to sit and brew a gloomy mood.
Some Buddhist followers, because of their disappointment
with the world, sit in melancholy, following the guidance
that always tells the world, "life is empty, life is not worthy."
As they sit there and think about it, they become more and
more devitalized.

The motivation or goal when you sit in meditation is
important. It suggests or channels you in the direction to
go, and then the boat will itself go in that direction. When
you sit, offer your cultivation to your joy, your spiritual
natural growth and so forth. If you decide that, the boat will
naturally go to that direction. If you do not suggest something and you sit there, then surely you have already
programmed yourself for what happens by your subcon-
scious mind. People are all affected by their own mind; life
is mostly self-suggested. How you guide yourself and how
you motivate yourself in any behavior is important.

Calming down is also important. Generally, when you
come back after work or after confusing social contacts, the
purpose of meditation is to put yourself back at peace and
in one piece. This means not to be scattered or disturbed
but to attain good concentration. Meditation lets the mind
take care of the spirit and lets the body take care of the
body. If you do not project a hope, there are no seeds and
you will grow nothing. Do you have a seed in your cultivation? Do you have a seed to cultivate spiritual energy? Use
the idea of natural spiritual truth as the goal or focus for
yourself; say to yourself that you wish to embrace the subtle
essence, attain the subtle essence, be as immortal as the
subtle essence and be as universal as the subtle essence.

Then you will achieve it. Such a thing is not questionable, so every day the wisdom grows.

Meditation must have a goal or purpose. If there is no purpose, then the meditation will have no purpose. For example, rice can be cooked as rice and also can be made into wine. Rice can also be made to be as sour as vinegar or made into cakes. If you do not have a purpose, then the rice does not know what you wish to do with it. It will end up staying there in a pot, just uncooked rice.

What have you learned before about meditation?

Q: They said to concentrate on the breath.

Master Ni: This is one way, the breathing method. There are many ways of breathing. General breathing is just to calm you down. Then after you calm down, you should feel achieved and be happy. Some breathing methods invigorate you. You do the invigoration, and then you are done. As I mentioned, whatever direction you go in, after you attain the goal, you should be happy. For example, if I take a half-hour walk, the walk has no special purpose, but walking itself can give a person strength just as meditation does. Sometimes the strength is subtle; by this I mean, it grows slowly and a person may not even be aware that it is there.

For example, one person meditates every day, and another person plays cards each day. The spiritual sensitivity will be different for the person who meditates each day for a half hour and the one who plays cards or does some other busy-minded activity. Spiritual sensitivity cannot be measured, but it develops slowly from meditation.

So it is important not to program yourself or sit there like some unhappy thing has happened or give yourself an unhappy thought. That is all dangerous. That emotional tendency can be corrected by giving yourself a fine day. With good weather in your meditation, it can be nothing like what is told as spiritual fantasy, but it is a fine day. So let your session of meditation at least be a fine day. There are other highly obtained goals, but they take longer. You must have a goal. If you do not have a goal, you cannot achieve anything. First you set your goal, then you ask what you should do to achieve it.

If you have no goal, I cannot decide your goal for you. I can only decide the method of how you reach your goal. I am the teacher, I am not you. The goal is what you decide. So think about your goal, then say you wish to reach the goal. What in my meditation is the content of my spirituality? You must improve your purposeless meditation or you must understand the purpose of meditative sitting. Then you reach the goal. That is important in spiritual practice.

Q: What kind of goals are you talking about?

Master Ni: Mental transcendence, the integration of personal energy, the Heavenly Eye, red baby and so forth.

Q: Isn't that ambition?

Master Ni: Ambition is a psychological strength if correctly applied. A correct spiritual goal is reasonable. It is not forceful ambition. It is not ambition at all. It is uprising energy. If there is no spiritual goal, then you do not need to do spiritual cultivation. In doing cultivation, one should discipline oneself not to rush the flowering. That will cause you trouble. Let the time be right for it to happen. This is why a person should have the ambition for spiritual cultivation but not be ambitious to project the result or achieve in one day.

You have to make up your mind. Some goals can be achieved in a shorter period. The practice of a breathing system can make you strong in three to six months. That is a way to learn. Internal energy conduction takes place at a more subtle level. If you learn the popular orbit circulation, you will not find the depth like you would in the above. Allow your bodily function to be natural to reach the depth of internal energy alchemy. Truthful achievement is unknown to those who have not reached the truth.

In learning immortal meditation, there must be some proof you attain; that is also the way to learn. There are many achievements and secrets of spiritual achievements.

The teacher may not teach someone who is unfit to learn. Such things are valuable. Some involve high secrets, but if you are really sincere in learning, then achievement comes sooner or later. As I say, it is like cooking rice, brewing wine or making vinegar; they all take a careful process to make something happen.

For example, sometimes I do T'ai Chi exercise, but sometimes I do not do it. In doing T'ai Chi, do I set a goal? Doing T'ai Chi exercise itself is a goal. The exercise itself is beneficial because it circulates the energy. On one level, it disperses the congestion from the head into the four limbs. There are other essential spiritual purposes that can be combined with T'ai Chi practice as well. T'ai Chi is a gentle way with a coordinating purpose.

If you wish to be an expert and have a special achievement, you have to have a special cultivation. If you would like to be a healer or have some other type of achievement when you are young and have lots of ambition, you may try this and that with some success. Then you move in a new direction. Know that true spiritual development is a boundless, unlimited way to go. It is not like religious belief in which one becomes a follower and it is not required to achieve anything.

There are some important goals and some unimportant goals. Some can be achieved and fulfilled in a short term, and some take a whole lifetime. When you are young and you go to a teacher, the teacher often asks, "What do you wish to learn, or what is your purpose?" After saying the purpose, such as you wish to learn spiritual practice, the teacher knows whether he is the right teacher for you and you are at the right stage. That is simple; you have a goal. Some things can be attained through meditation and some things can be obtained through other methods of learning. Different goals require different means of achievement.

You have to be clear about yourself. A young person has so much potential. Under Heaven, no one should underestimate a young person. A young person who has ambition, if he finds the right teacher or right way, in a number of years will achieve himself to be totally different from how you first saw or judged him.

General students do not know how to order.   For example, if someone goes to a Chinese restaurant, he does not know how to order if he is not highly experienced in eating Chinese food. Only the experts know the best dishes. Some restaurants are ordinary; they mostly serve the same thing and arrange it a little differently.   Basically, I teach young people who do not know anything about spiritual reality. Spiritually, they do not know how to ask. So they need to carefully study my books, find the point and circle or underline the parts that interest them the most. Then, as they keep reading my other books, they will come back to those parts to break through. This is the best learning, the simplest learning.

Modern people do not have time to follow a teacher for twenty or thirty years or stay in a spiritual place to learn a lot or study. Also, there are very few good books in English. If you learn from reading my books, and you absorb my experience, then you have an achievement equal to mine. So some people, just by sitting in a chair, can obtain all my achievement that came through a lot of hard work. I myself had to go through all the difficulties to be able to do all this writing for my wise readers.

Q: Is seeing visions the result of sexual energy rising into the head and being transformed into images? How is seeing visions different from the Heavenly Eye? Also, how is seeing visions different from the subtle light?

Master Ni: Energy rising into the head and transforming into images is different from the Heavenly Eye. The Heavenly Eye is a special achieved vision. There are also several kinds of Heavenly Eye which are functionally different. For example, one kind of Heavenly Eye can see treasures under the ocean. Another kind is a message that shows the energy information from inside and outside to give you a different understanding from the one in your mind. So from your image and the vision, you can discern the reality of a circumstance; practically speaking, it is the correction of the mind.   The mind works through doubt, deduction and conclusion; so many processes. The vision of the Heavenly

Eye presents the message or information instantly and directly. The image tells you.

When a person's energy rises into the head, it causes congestion and affects one's vision, so the person sees things differently. That is nothing compared to the Heavenly Eye. The Heavenly Eye is opened through long cultivation. It opens from pure energy, not the energy of the body which rises to the head in a strong flow with blood. There is a difference. It is the refined chi which crystallizes, and feels subtly like ethereal spiritual particles. They are also very effective; they can help the Heavenly Eye.

Seeing true visions is really different from energy rising into the head and being transferred into images. People also see visions in dreams. Generally speaking, people are in a trance during some part of their dream when they receive a message. This is not high achievement, because all people see visions in dreams. The visions of most people are not reflections of reality at all; they are mostly twisted, because they are associated with a person's psychological experience.

There is such a thing as a true vision. It happens during a person's meditation or cultivation when he is deeply relaxed, not in sleep. Few people are born with this natural gift. In order to obtain a vision, usually the eyes are half closed, and a vision occurs. The subject matter of a true vision is spiritual in nature. Usually it is controllable. Visions of this type can be controlled or enhanced by being in a room that is not too bright, rather than in an open, very bright room. This is the truth. It needs cultivation to reach it; it is not like general visions.

The gift of seeing visions is a spiritual achievement. Others see them just because their energy is weak. Some people see visions because their mind is confused. There are many reasons for seeing visions. Some visions can be used to help oneself in a positive way. Some visions do not help, though, so it is important to always remember, no matter what vision is seen, to keep up your spiritual practice and your good concentration in daily life. Treat it as though nothing happened. That is important. If you see a Heavenly being, or if God or Buddha comes to you, do not be overly happy about it. It could be mostly false. Also, if you see a bad thing and you feel bad, do not dwell on it, but maintain your habitual calmness. If you are achieved enough, you can use the message from your vision. That is achievement, too, that comes through growth. It is always important to maintain your composure in whatever vision you are seeing.

The subtle light is different from visions. The subtle light is the solution or direct spiritual guidance for a problem you have.

Q: Is refinement when a person's sexual energy rises in his body? Does the refinement happen by itself as the energy rises? It sounds like it is not really something that a person does, it just happens after one changes his habits so that he does not lose a lot of energy through too much sex, thought, emotion or worldly attraction. Does the rising itself refine the energy?

Master Ni: This question asks if sexual energy automatically rises. For the most part, people are generally calm and at peace sexually unless something happens to stimulate them such as a suggestive movie, pornographic magazine or sexual conversation. Then a reaction is stirred and the sexual organ becomes stimulated.

The rising of the sexual energy also depends on the type of work a person does and whether he or she knows the special technique to refine the sexual energy. If the person is a spiritual person and lives a life of work that is connected with uplifting spiritual energy, the person is benefitted.

There are many books published that are mostly for sexual interest. Young people read them and immediately the energy from their head area goes down. It is easy to see how good energy from a calm, normal mind transforms into sexual energy. Even a person of spiritual awareness or spiritual sensitivity responds to such stimulation. Thus, they choose good stimulation instead of reading that would pull them down. They know that it is also hard not to let that part of their energy be disturbed by such stimulation. The best and safest way is to maintain the energy in the normal place. Without such thoughts, or by not having one's vision stimulated, the energy will not go to the lower region and transform into sexual energy before it is completely sublimated.

In a normal situation, the energy is neutral. It is not mental energy, sexual energy or spiritual energy. I can make an analogy of energy to gasoline which can be used for driving a car, starting a lawn mower or heating a swimming pool. Before it is used, the gasoline is just gasoline. Surely human energy is much more subtle, higher and more precious than that, but it still can be applied and transformed differently.

When a person's sexual energy automatically rises, the transmutation can be done by reading spiritual books, but I am talking about good spiritual books, worthy of time and energy. Religious books can make a person excited to move their energy to a different end, because they generally stir one's emotion. Bodily energy transmutation can also be done by art work. This is called transferring the bodily energy from one level to another. If it is systematically practiced, it is the sublimation of physical energy. Sublimation means to take the general energy through refinement to rise to a higher level of spiritual energy.

You mentioned that you thought it was not really something that a person has to do. However, a person should maintain discipline and stay alert to when the energy drops down there. That is something to do.

In ancient times, people who worked on farms looked much healthier, both men and women. This is because they were not overly stimulated by doing that type of work. Their internal energy was undisturbed. They were supported for the most part by their own healthy energy, so they were different from other people who live in an unnatural environment.

Q: Master Ni, the conception of a spiritual baby does not make any sense to me. If a person is going to attain the subtle essence, why does he need to create a new spiritual body? If you achieve yourself spiritually, you dissolve everything, don't you?

Master Ni: The spiritual baby is a new yourself. You will experience yourself and say, I am real and alive; then you plunge yourself into the subtle essence. That is the shien level. The shien level is different from other things. A shien can form oneself any time or dissolve oneself, without going through the general physical life and death. They totally follow their free will and form themselves according to the situation. A shien is just like a piece of special energy.

That kind of achievement may not interest you, but I still think it is a most practical and provable step. Though a spiritual student should not be attached to anything, a little proof is more realistic than ideology.

Q: What does the subtle light look like? Sometimes when I sit, I see a soft purple light that comes before me in varying intensities and then fades away. I believe it was my sexual energy transforming as thoughts and then escaping. Am I correct?

Master Ni: You are a young woman with good spiritual discipline and a strong spiritual ambition to achieve yourself. You have been doing spiritual cultivation for a long time and I believe that your life condition is suitable for spiritual cultivation. You must live in a quiet, nice, natural surrounding. You especially keep good sexual discipline; you are almost celibate. I believe that every day you have contact with and keep studying the high spiritual books and teachings. So you have the opportunity to witness this high frequency light.

At the spiritual level, there is precious light. It is far higher than transformed sexual energy that goes through a refining process from red, yellow, white, light blue, deep blue and then becomes purple. It could be your own attainment. It could be also the divine energy come to approach you.

High experience is hard to keep. You still have psychology, emotion, worldly pressure and family members which need your attention. All these things should be carefully handled without letting them turn into negative influences. If you keep doing well, the next step is that you might see the images and hear the voices of high spiritual beings who are interested in helping you by advising and instructing you as subtly as the light you saw. If you are too rough, though, then you come down to live on a different level, and you will never have a chance to contact the subtle level. Your further achievement is your responsibility. But be careful, do not hold a strong expectation for spiritual phenomena or reality to be presented to you; this happens in a subtle, delicate way. The general approach has no use on such an occasion. Keep reading my books or any good books; you might be guided somewhere. Usually they are safe; the energy arrangement in all my work is a garden of high spiritual reality.

Spiritual achievement is like planting flowers and arranging a flower garden. The really hard work is keeping the weeds out. Before, when you had no flower and no garden, you did not see the weeds. After you have flowers and a garden, everything suddenly changes: the weeds are as noticeable as the flowers. They are annoying and destructive to the beauty of the flowering plant. They are like a cancer. You must remember to protect your beautiful garden from weeds. The flowers do not demand too much time; mostly they grow naturally, just by living in a suitable environment. Keep in mind that it takes you more time to constantly clear the weeds out of your garden. Once the weeds are out, the flowers and the crops will naturally grow in their own way.

After it is stronger, spiritual energy can be light, image and voice. A spiritual person who is serious in doing his spiritual cultivation has no desire whatsoever for any kind of excitement. You still make mistakes because the mind can hardly be together with the spirits all the time. It has its habitual way of doing things; then troubles and small mistakes keep coming back, so subtly that nobody else knows it. You are upset by mistakes. Who tells you about the mistakes you have made? Your effective, responsive, reflecting spirit tells you that you are wrong. You do not appreciate who tells that you made a mistake. Then, what is the use of those years you have done of spiritual cultivation? However, pride of mind starts even when a person is a teenager. People think they know a lot, but they stay ignorant out of mental pride even when they are quite old. Because your defect of the mind is pride, assertiveness, stubbornness and inconsiderateness, you carry the trouble over and over, lifetime after lifetime. To do spiritual cultivation, you almost do not need to do anything, just sit in the right direction and you will be there. However, you will never be there unless you correct the pride of your mind, the instability, assertiveness, inconsiderateness, haste and prejudice of being born into a different gender, race, society, culture and religion than the pure energy of the natural mind. All those things forge a strong shackle for your mind. So after you dissolve yourself, dissolve the mind and totally unite with the spiritual energy, then you are the way, the light, the truth and the god. There will be no cross on your shoulder, no crucifixion, no humiliation, no thorny crown to wear on your head. Your dream will be fulfilled beautifully, not fulfilled in a negative way. A God born with the effect of the mind suffers from worldly problems and becomes a particular model of worldly ordeals. Those things will not happen to you if you receive the correct growth.

Chapter 4

Instruction for
Effective Spiritual Cultivation

This chapter commemorates the contribution of Master Kou Hong as a good example for later realizers or students of natural spiritual truth.

Tsing Jing Ching, or "Guidance to Purity"

This spiritual instruction was said to have been handed down from Master Kou Shuan, the Immortal (164 - ? A.D.). He received it from his teacher, Master Tso Tzu, the Immortal, who appeared and made fun of the usurper Tsao Tsao (155-220 A.D.).

1. The Ageless Master said, The Integral Truth has no physical form, yet it keeps forming the universe. The Integral Truth has no self-intention, yet it moves all, making the sun and moon, etc., revolve as they do.

    The Integral Truth claims no name but nourishes the growth of all things.

    Although it has no name, people named it. Some called it the Integral Way, or Great Path.

2. Subtle Universal Energy expresses itself through two types of energy or things. The two types are classified as yang and yin. Yang is whatever is light and pure, and yin is whatever is heavy and impure. Also, yang is motion, and yin is inertia.

    The sky is in motion; thus, it is yang energy. The earth is concrete; thus, it is yin energy. Therefore, motion or force is yang and solid forms or things of concretion are yin.

    The universe as we know it is composed of these two main types of energy, yin and yang. Just like the universe, an individual also contains yin and yang energy. An individual of spiritual cultivation who knows about yin and yang allows each to perform its natural function. In this way, the person achieves harmony and peace both inside the body and outside in the environment.

3.   The internal energy of each individual has different positions and functions.   However, an overactive mind disturbs the orderliness of this energy. The mind of people may think that it loves peace, but its own emotion and desire draw it away from the very peace it seeks. If a person could end one's emotion and desire, the mind would become peaceful by itself. When the mind is free of desire and emotion and is clean, a person's spiritual energy will of itself become pure and effective in serving the life of that person.

When a person's mind is clean and spiritual energy is pure and effective, then desire and emotion will no longer arise.

4. The reason why people are not able to attain purity of mind is because their minds have not been cleansed, and their desires have not been sent away.

If one is able to eliminate desire and emotion, one is no longer confused when one looks in toward one's mind. Similarly, when the mind is pure, one is no longer confused when one looks out at the body. Also with a pure mind, when one looks farther, at external things in the world, one knows that those things are all trouble and one has nothing to do with them.

When one understands these things, one will see only purity. This purity will awaken the depth of purity which is the essence in the depth of life. In the depth of purity is the essence of life. It is one's spiritual energy. Without such depth, no essence is reached.

When the mind is pure, the being is quiet. In a quiet being, there no longer exists an unconscious inner conflict of wishing that occupied space would be vacant space. In a quiet being, there no longer exists an unconscious inner conflict of wishing that somethingness would be nothingness. In a quiet being, all conflicting conceptions, conscious and unconscious, have disappeared, and the condition of serenity or inner peace is reached.

5. In that condition of peace which exists independently of all conceptual conflict, no desire can arise, not even the desire to get rid of desires. When no desire on any level whatsoever arises, all that exists is the True Pure Mind.

The True Pure Mind can become a constant spiritual quality. It responds to external things without error. That True and Constant quality holds possession of the deep spiritual nature.

During the constant challenges of daily life and constant response by the mind, there is a constant unity between challenge and response. The mind of the person with True Pure Mind remains in constant unity with deep spiritual nature.

The person who has attained unity with deep spiritual nature has become united with the integral truth of the universe. And having entered the spiritual core of the universe, one is becoming the spiritual truth of the universe.

After a person has realized the Integral Truth, that person does not think that he has taken possession of any great spiritual power of nature. Becoming the spiritual truth of the universe is different from the transformation that happens to all living things, the falling away from the center. One who is able to understand this may transmit the truth of eternal life to others.

6. The Ageless Master said, The highest achieved ones do not strive for anything. Those who possess great spiritual power do not show it.

People who have not accomplished their spiritual development are fond of striving. People who possess shallow knowledge of universal spiritual reality hold tightly to their concentrated beliefs, and display and impose them upon others. Those who so tightly hold and display them are not harmonious with spiritual reality and its attributes of nature.

7. The reason why all people do not reach the Integral Truth is because their minds are affected, twisted, confused or perverted by the world. Their minds being perverted, their spirits become perturbed. Because their minds are

perturbed, they are attracted toward external things and greedily begin seeking those things. This greedy quest leads to perplexities and annoyances; and these again result in disordered thoughts, which cause anxiety and trouble in both body and mind. Such people then meet with foul play or disgrace. Their lives and deaths have a wild character and they tend to sink in the sea of bitterness. They lose the opportunity to realize the Integral Truth of Eternal Life.

8. The True and Abiding Integral Way! Those who understand it naturally obtain it. Those who come to understand the Integral Truth of life abide in purity and unity.

The Avoidance of Self-Entrapment

On other occasions, I have described some of my personal experiences which seem to be useful and fascinating for my readers. One important point I would like to make about the interesting things that I described is that a student of the Integral Truth knows never to cherish a fanciful thought in his mind. If he does, he will be misled by such thoughts and will not reach a realistic goal or true achievement. If someone doing spiritual cultivation is full of imagination and illusions, the person will have trouble in the world and doing cultivation.

The things I have described were experiences of my personal stages of growth. They were not my goal. Spiritual cultivation is practical and down to earth. It is closely related to one's daily life and one's movement in the world. If a person is not realistic about himself and his goal of spiritual cultivation, practically, he will fall into "Satan's trap." Satan is his own mind! The mind causes or suggests problems for oneself. The one practicing spiritual cultivation can learn to solve his problems by learning to adjust his mind and by putting his interest in internal and external improvement.

In the process of one's cultivation, many interesting things can happen. The few things that I have described are just a small part. However, even though they are interesting because they are unusual, it is hardly even worth talking about them. They are not worthy to consider as a pursuit. When they happen - and if you are serious on this path, things like this will happen - you calmly accept them as only one other phenomenon or experience that passes by.

So the experiences I have described, even though they are real, are only something that passes by. Those short-lived things are not the eternal truth. Maybe they are just a little entertainment on the way there. Phenomena always pass. A true realizer of integral spiritual truth never turns back to what has passed. The reason the realizer of truth does not turn back is that experiencing phenomena is not the purpose of spiritual cultivation.

Spiritual cultivation, at its highest level, has two purposes that can be described. One purpose or goal is to achieve what I call "Absolute Spirit." I would like to give you an example or description of this, because it is important to understand.

You may have noticed that sometimes in your daily life you experience happiness and excitement. Usually you are glad when those things happen. But on the other hand, it cannot be avoided that sometimes you also experience pain, disappointment or agony. So, you always have dualistic experiences: good and bad, long and short, left and right. All those things are presented to you or enter your aware-ness in a dualistic pattern. If a person accepts or believes that life is that way and nothing can be done about it, his spirit will be split in half by those two divisions. He will experience his life as always up and down, left and right. It will seem that he can never be straight or touch the point.

However, there is a way out of that dizzying motion of duality. Once you achieve absolute spirit, you are no longer on the level of playing yo-yo, going up and down over and over again. You will stabilize your life, stay in the center and reach the target. When you stay in the bull's eye of the target, you do not scatter your energy any more by moving up and down. You stay where things are sharp and clear: in the center. That is what I call the absolute spirit. It is above the experience of the relative sphere of happiness or pain. It is above the level of playing success and failure in the world. It is above the level of emotional rises and falls.

Those things still exist, but they do not have a great effect, because they are no longer very important.

The second purpose of spiritual cultivation is what I call "All Embracing Spirit." Once you achieve yourself to the top of the level of beingness, including the spirits, you reach the absolute. A different wording is the ultimate truth. Once you reach the first principle, the ultimate truth, you become the one of the universe. You are the one who can produce or create anything. You are the one who embraces the entirety of nature. However, as one who embraces the entirety of the universe and nature, you are not partial. This also means that you are not bothered, pulled away or repelled by one small or big element. You always encompass and include everything. This I describe as all embracing spirit. For this, a student of the Integral Way pursues and cultivates himself.

Individual experiences, both good and bad, always help to build you so that you can go one step further. With regard to one's experiences, there is nothing worthy of attachment.

In order to help the trouble that types of sitting meditation would cause, a person can learn and practice physical arts. For example, gentle movement such as Chi Kung (Chi Gong) or T'ai Chi can lift a person out of his own psychological or spiritual pitfall. I would like to talk more about T'ai Chi movement and internal energy exercise and how they can assist one's spiritual development.

Building a Balanced Life through Balanced Cultivation

Q: Master Ni, it sounds like Absolute Spirit is when a person who is used to sitting on one end of a rapidly moving seesaw changes his position and moves to the center of it. He is no longer affected by its continuing, rough movements because he is at the balance point. He learns that it is nicer to sit in the center of the seesaw because he is not bounced around so much. It is calmer, and besides, sometimes the motion at the ends made him feel a little sick to his stomach.

It sounds like All Embracing Spirit is when he sits there calmly in the center. After he settles himself and his stomach down by sitting there for some time, he is a little bored at first, but then he begins to look around. Soon he is aware that there is a whole park surrounding him and people participating in other activities, a beautiful lake with geese and many trees and a clear blue sky. As he sits there, he can see all of the activity and beauty, thus he embraces all of it. Yet when he was on the seesaw, he could only be aware of his own bouncing up and down, and his own emotional reactions to that game. Does that come close to describing spiritual achievement, or is that still only the emotional level (i.e., calming down a general type of life, and not yet approaching any true spiritual growth)?

Master Ni: What you described is a good place to start.

Now I would like to talk about holistic spiritual cultivation. The visible part of self-cultivation is the bodily energy conducting which is exemplified by T'ai Chi Chuan or Chi exercise. (Hereafter I use the words, "Gentle Movement" or "Internal Arts" to include the whole system of physical-spiritual cultivation.) The secret of spiritual cultivation is to cultivate the two sides of one's nature in a balanced way: both the sitting still type of cultivation and the active moving type of cultivation. Gentle movement or T'ai Chi exercise was initiated after spiritual educators emphasized an inactive, quiet sitting and an inactive, quiet life. Let us start by reviewing the two most important elements of gentle movement: body and spirits. People who wish to live a healthy life or who wish to learn the Integral Way keep their bodies active. By your activity, you are always generating new energy. In addition, activity increases your circulation and regulates your system. If your movement or physical activity is not overdone, it is always helpful. That is physical law. How much activity or exercise is proper for a person depends on his or her age and physical condition.

The opposite of being active is resting or sleeping. That is also an important topic, but some people have mistaken ideas about it. Some people think that sleeping for a long time will make them become stronger. I have seen some athletes or sports people who can sleep nonstop for three days if they are not disturbed. I had a friend who was a boxing champion and very vigorous in the arena who could sleep for several days at a time, but despite his athletic strength, his physical condition was very poor, so he died young. If either side, activity or sleep, is extreme, a person will not be benefitted in the broad sense.

Knowing this helps us recognize that physically we need movement in order to enliven our lives. This we might call the physical law.

Spiritual cultivation is the opposite of physical law. In spiritual cultivation, keeping quiet or keeping still gathers a person's energy. Restless movement or purposeless activity especially scatters one's energy. Most people, especially those who live in cities, participate in this type of restless movement or purposeless activity. This is why so often I recommend that people be calm, live a quiet life and practice sitting cultivation. In that way, a person's energy will gather.

Some older people are still active and travel a lot; mostly that helps their emotions. They do not have a spiritual goal of gathering their energy to become an everlasting spiritual life. They do not expect that nor do they know that it exists, so on the day when their physical essence ends, their energy scatters and the person will become a ghost or reincarnate again.

A Spiritually Channelled Life

A spiritual person lives his life differently. His life is more focused because he is engaging in a spiritual enterprise. He is following the principle of accumulation by saving, just like putting money in a bank in the capitalist system. He is constantly depositing energy in his own spiritual "bank." He is not scattered by wandering or fooling around, traveling widely or chasing any wild geese. By doing that, gently, unconsciously, his energy stays in the same natural environment. The natural environment supports your energy. If you live in a city, you are supported by city conveniences. A spiritually focused person nurtures his spirits, so that in the future he achieves an

SEVEN STAR
COMMUNICATIONS
G R O U P

Please send me information on the following:

☐ Books and tapes for spiritual realization, practical self healing and Taoist Movement arts.

☐ Los Angeles area health clinics encompassing Acupuncture, Chinese Herbs and Nutrition offering high quality service at low cost.

☐ A 4-year professional training program leading to a Masters Degree of Acupuncture and Traditional Chinese Medicine.

☐ Chinese regenerative herbal foods for health and longevity.

☐ A business opportunity with a great product and plan.

Name _____

Address _____

City _____ State _____ Zip _____

Book in which you found this card: _____

SEVEN STAR
COMMUNICATIONS
G R O U P
1314 SECOND STREET
SANTA MONICA, CA 90401 USA

everlasting spiritual life in a different sphere. At that time, he surpasses life and death.

Forms Bring No Limitation but Understanding

Spiritual cultivation means many things. In general, it means the attainment of enlightenment. That is beneficial. Sometimes it also means attaining confidence in living life; that is also beneficial. A higher level is reaching a sphere where life and death are no longer a problem. A person engaging in higher development passes through stages of biological or physical growth, psychological or mental growth, and development of psychic energy or powers. Those powers are also beneficial, but they are a secondary achievement.

All realistic achievement comes through accumulation. There is no other way. This is why we need to live a harmonious, gentle, quiet and subtle life. Or we need to have quiet time in the midst of an active life. In that way, we can gently and subtly gather the high essence to form the new baby that is born into the spiritual sphere. That is the everlasting sphere. It is not a belief; it is a realization that is accomplished through cultivation. Without cultivation, one will never achieve that reality.

Many people believe it. They agree that such a thing exists, and have no problem accepting it. You know, for example, that there is Peking, Rome and New York. Perhaps you have never been to those places, but you believe that they exist. How do you really know that they exist if you have not been there? I encourage people to go past the level of belief and have some experience.

However, spiritual learning is different from traveling from one city to another. If you go to those places, you find that they are cities just like any other city. Perhaps some small external details are different. I have given this example to show that people believe that if they keep traveling they will find something different from where they already are. Spiritual cultivation is not traveling; it is merely going deeper into where you already are. It is a matter of staying quietly where you are and experiencing more subtle levels of your own being.

The main point of this discussion is that physical law and spiritual law seem to conflict with each other. Physical law is to keep moving, because vigorous moving will invigorate your life energy. On the other hand, spiritual law is to stay calm and quiet, because stillness will gather your spiritual energy. Each law goes a different way. However, these two laws are ultimately not conflicting. Let us go further.

The Practice of Singular Mental Control Is Fruitless

During the Sung Dynasty (960-1279 A.D.), there was a great scholar named Wahn Geng Chai. He was born in Wenchow, which is also my hometown. He was a highly disciplined person and a renowned scholar. He believed that absolute control of the mind was the way of a sage. Therefore, he was never distracted by anything; he always kept moving forward in his discipline. He never talked much about anything else; mostly he only spoke when it was necessary. He put himself in complete concentration. Unfortunately, one thing he neglected was exercise, so he died in his 30s.

His example shows us how we need to find a spiritual and physical way to eliminate the conflict between the two laws. How do we do that? By combining them. During Wahn's time, people were only taught how to conduct their energy through sitting meditation. Up to his time, in the long history of seekers of eternal life, no way had yet been found to combine both physical and spiritual laws into one. How can stillness and movement be harmonized? People recognized that both were needed, but their solution was to alternate, so there was still a division. For one hour, a person did some moving. The moving was according to physical law but against spiritual law, so during the second hour, the person would sit. This would help him spiritually but not physically.

So what ended the dilemma? One principle of T'ai Chi states that when movement comes to its extreme, it gives birth to stillness, and when stillness comes to its extreme, it gives birth to movement. Movement exists in stillness, and stillness exists in movement. Neither of them is an absolute stage. They not only give birth to each other, they express and suggest the opposite in any single moment of expression.

T'ai Chi is the ultimate truth of life.   The T'ai Chi principle points to the unsettled problem of whether movement or stillness is spiritual. As you know, the T'ai Chi principle expresses both yin and yang, daytime and nighttime, so some teachers set up half of the day to be quiet and the other half for moving around. Because that was not accurate enough, after long years of demand, T'ai Chi Chuan was developed.   It combines both stillness and movement. What does the word "chuan" mean? Chuan means a set of movements. Usually it means martial art, but now I correct it to mean gentle physical movement or Chi Kung practice.

Use Gentle Physical Movement to Assist Physical Health and the Development of Individual Life

When you do gentle movement, you are moving, yet at the same time you experience quietude, inner stillness, calmness and composure. Gentle movement combines all good spiritual virtues with the benefit of physical exercise. This great harmonization became gentle movement or T'ai Chi movement.

Now I would like to talk about the position of Gentle Movement or internal energy movement in spiritual self-cultivation, spiritual self-integration or subtle self-integration of a new life. I have already explained to you that there are steps to achieving immortality or creating a "red" immortal baby.   The first step is to refine one's general nutrition from food or air to become one's physical essence. This physical essence is sexual energy, because people have an animal foundation in their beingness. Sexual energy, in our terms, is called "ching."   So one's sexual energy is nurtured by the food one eats and one's breathing.

The next step is to refine the sexual energy to be a higher sphere of energy called chi. Many people do not understand chi; later I will talk about it because it is so important. The next step is to take the chi and refine it to a higher, more subtle energy called "sen" in Chinese. The next step is to gather the sen; from this gathering, the spiritual conception is accomplished. The spiritual conception brings about a red baby or angel for your new life. We call it a red baby as an analogy of a newborn baby whose skin is still pink or red. The energy of the newly created immortal life is symbolized by the newness of a human baby.

All steps are important. Perhaps the middle part, of refining sexual energy into spiritual energy, and then changing the spiritual energy into the new life are the most challenging. Why? Because they require self-control over different aspects of your being. Sometimes it seems as though you are giving something up, although you are really gaining something.

One of the aspects of your being that you must control is your mind. The mind usually means one's emotions or psychology as affected by one's living conditions, environment and each individual's sexual energy. You may not yet know that, but all of these - emotions, psychology, living conditions, environment and energy - are controlled by the mind or left to run rampant if there is no self-respect or discipline. Close self-observation will show this to be true.

If a person learns how to control his mind, he can build up his sexual energy. So the next step is to refine the sexual energy to be chi. Now I need to give you a secret. I would like to tell you how to do it. Let me begin by first going deeper.

Chi has multiple functions. One apparent, easily seen function is immunity. For example, if a person has strong chi, it means that the person does not easily become sick. In general, when people catch a cold, it is because the person's immune system is low; thus, he can easily be attacked by a virus. On the other hand, if the person's immunity is strong, then even if there is a flu going around, he will not catch it. This is one function of chi.

However, colds are caught for different reasons. If a person has sudden changes in hot and cold, it can be a reason to catch a cold, but that is not related to chi, that is different. We are talking about the immune energy that is called "wei chi." A person's wei chi will be low, for example, if he allows himself to be very tired over a long period of time. Low wei chi is usually caused by poor living habits.

A person who does Gentle Movement or internal energy movement is able to transfer his sexual energy into wei chi to enhance his or her immune system. This is why practitioners of T'ai Chi do not easily get a cold; their chi flows smoothly throughout the whole body. And this is an interesting thing. If a person who has been practicing Gentle Movement for an extended period of time has sex, he might easily catch a cold the next day. Why? Because chi is something so subtle. It moves between the skin and muscle and can protect a person, but having sex can break the strength of the protection. It can take the chi away from protecting the person, kind of like a leak or damage caused. People who do not do Gentle Movement such as T'ai Chi or Chi Kung and have sex are not sensitive to this. They may not catch colds, but they will become run down physically over an extended period of time. It is not that doing T'ai Chi or Chi Kung will make you catch colds. It is only the sudden change of direction of the chi that caused the problem for the T'ai Chi person or Chi Kung practitioner.

In my tradition, there is some important guidance that I will tell you. First I would like to explain a few things. When you practice Gentle Movement such as T'ai Chi or Chi Kung, you unconsciously increase chi. However, you may not know about it or notice it until you have sex and catch a cold. You think to yourself, why did I get a cold? The answer is that the chi was lost in sexual activity. A T'ai Chi or Chi Kung practitioner can experience this. An ordinary person has no way to tell how he got a cold, but the T'ai Chi or Chi Kung practitioner will know that he got a cold from sex.

In ancient times, a teacher of T'ai Chi Chuan or other chi exercise would also instruct his students in push hands. Push hands is dual T'ai Chi practice. When a person does push hands, the most important thing is his concentration. If you match up two people of equal skill, the one who does not do as well is the one who had sex the night before. His concentration is not as good because the energy was pulled away from his brain. If you learn push hands, you can test this and learn for yourself that sexual activity drains the chi.

I am leading up to telling you the valuable guidance of the ancestors. Their advice was not to be celibate and hide from the opposite sex by living in a cave. Many people who cultivated themselves then, just as now, were married people and had obligations. However, if they wished to have sexual activity, three days beforehand they would stop their practice and become an ordinary person. Then, after sex, they would wait for four days before resuming their T'ai Chi Chuan or Chi Kung practice to restore the normalcy of their energy flow. This is called "chien sang houz" - three days before, four days after. I am glad to have the opportunity to explain this principle to you and to all people so that they can understand and better control their paired or single life situation, rather than going to live in caves.

When a person knows that he would like to maintain a high level of chi rather than have sex, he has broken through one of the great mental obstructions to realizing the Integral Truth. It is passing through a great checkpoint. When a person practices T'ai Chi or Chi Kung and sees the potential or opportunity for personal achievement, and knows that it is better than anything else, he finally learns to stop strong sexual desire. Once you refine that kind of desire, then you can easily break through that obstruction.

People without interest in spiritual life will experience that their T'ai Chi or Chi Kung practice enhances and enforces their sexual capability. There are descriptions of sexual fantasy that many people can only think about, but people who practice internal energy exercises such as T'ai Chi or Chi Kung can actually fulfill them. Their practice will give them a special capability. A rarely achieved master, doing sexual meditation with the right partner, can last seven days continually without an ejaculation and still be strong. My personal experience is that a person's sexual energy is much increased by T'ai Chi or Chi Kung practice. However, many excellent T'ai Chi champions or teachers died young by transferring that power into the fulfillment of sexual fantasies. I do not recommend sexual fantasy as a pursuit, only as a test for your own proof that it is true. If you test it and find that you have that capability, it means that your control over your nervous system is much stronger than that of most people.

In achieving spiritual immortality, most people recognize, as I also did through my personal experience, that refining sexual energy into chi is the second step. My personal experience of T'ai Chi or Chi Kung practice is that when combined with other instruction, it can take you step by step toward the goal of immortality. The practice of Gentle Movement can be useful in all the steps. By the way, during the second stage of refining one's energy toward immortal life, not only does a person refine his sexual energy into chi. One's sexual energy, mental energy and physical energy all integrate through T'ai Chi or Chi Kung practice to become chi.

I have mentioned the steps or realistic way to achieve immortality. The place of difficulty for many people is this part. It is not hard to learn a system and transfer one's sexual energy into chi, but it is hard to maintain chi to become sen. Sen is much more subtle. You can find the way to nurture it in the *Tao Teh Ching*.

So many T'ai Chi or Chi Kung teachers are in a stage where their chi is very strong, but they use it, for example, in sex or fighting. If they do not waste their chi in sexual recreation or fighting, then in their push hands movement, a gentle touch from them can make a strong man lose his balance and fall four or five yards away. How can the person have such a power? It is not physical force; it is the gathering of chi that can do that.

Many people who practice T'ai Chi or Chi Kung regularly and do not go deeply into understanding it use their accumulated energy in two spheres: either sex or push hands fighting. Other people, if they accumulate some energy, will discharge it in other ways - for example, in emotional outbursts - but if the person is a student of the Integral Way and is really seriously looking for spiritual immortality, he will not stay in the stage characterized by, "As a T'ai Chi practitioner, I am strong in fighting or in sex. That is all I need." The serious student goes from this step and utilizes his achieved chi and refines it into sen or spiritual energy.

Step by step, the possibility is there for immortality, so now I am releasing this secret to people who are learning. It is not hard to achieve spiritual immortality, it is hard to go through the checkpoint entitled "general sexual desire." If you stand there and do not pass, you are locked out from the sphere of spiritual immortality.

Let us continue to discuss more about Gentle Movement and other kinds of internal energy exercise.

T'ai Chi movement such as Chi Kung is based on the principle of harmony between yin and yang - two opposing forces. It is the main theme of the *I Ching* or *The Book of Changes and the Unchanging Truth.* Gentleness in movement and life is based on the elucidation of Lao Tzu's written work, the *Tao Teh Ching.* As you deepen your study of the *I Ching*, which is also called *The Book of Changes and the Unchanging Truth*, and continue to study the *Tao Teh Ching*, you can use the principles that you learn in your practice of T'ai Chi movement or other energy exercises.

Walking is another way to practice T'ai Chi, through the interplay of left and right legs. Also swinging the left and right arms is practicing T'ai Chi. Do not be confused. I do not promote any generation or school of T'ai Chi Chuan which lacks depth. I am talking purposely about Gentle Movement which is closely connected with one's conscious mind as a unison. It is not a separate conducting and exercise. In this book or on other occasions I have given the special set of movements in meditation. How a practitioner uses his or her T'ai Chi practice depends on the level of spiritual attainment.

The *I Ching* and the *Tao Teh Ching* are two important teachings in the ancient teaching of the Integral Way. During the end of the Tang Dynasty, a great sage was born. That was a time when society was confused. He did not earn a position as ruler or adviser to a ruler, but he contributed to the peace of China during that period of history by guiding young people to achieve it. He was Master Chen Tuan. I will introduce him to you in the second volume. Also, by his profound study of the *I Ching*, he refreshed the vision of all the Confucian scholars and brought about the reintegration of Taoism and Confucianism.

The practice of T'ai Chi Chuan was started by Master Zhan, San Fong, a realizer of the natural spiritual truth who received the influence of Master Chen Tuan, but with good spiritual development.   He lived in Wu Dang mountain where Master Chen Tuan lived in his early stage of his spiritual cultivation.   The T'ai Chi principle as ancient cosmology of integral spiritual vision can be credited to Master Chen Tuan. Around 100 years later, according to existing records, Master Zhan was inspired in a vision brought to him by a spiritual authority, a god of mystical Heaven, Shuan Ti. Master Zhan, San Fong or some other achieved one initiated the combination of quietude in movement.   He integrated both, so that where there is movement, there is stillness, and where there is calmness, there is activity.

Therefore, T'ai Chi Chuan is not just another program from somebody's intellectual mind; although it is told that it is the inspiration of spirits, I think it is a fruit of nature. It deeply integrates the principles of the *I Ching*.

Once I had an interesting experience. I got a cold, but I could not stop seeing patients because the appointments were already made. I was suffering from the cold and sat in my chair in the early morning. My vision started acting; I saw myself doing some sword dancing. Suddenly, I understood that doing sword dancing was the cure for my cold. So I did the sword dancing to force the virus out by a little sweating, got over the suffering and went back to work.

Similar inspiration comes to me, for my work, writing or other activities. A positive, busy minded person can always receive spiritual help if he is quietly listening for it. The attitude of rushing and haste always slows down the expected good harvest. All teachings given were also received in the same way.

In general, when you lay the foundation for your achievement, you will find that the easiest way to nurture the subtle energy is to practice Gentle Movement in a quiet place with no one else around. Why? It is helpful for better concentration. The other thing that is helpful is to always come back to read the *I Ching* and the *Tao Teh Ching* to correct your T'ai Chi movement. Your deeper and deeper understanding of those works will make your T'ai Chi movement more effective. It will also help you attain general health and even go as high as to help you attain your spiritual immortality.

Philosophy helps us understand better, but to realize the goal, Gentle Movement is a useful tool. It can help us reach our goal of spiritual immortality or at least attain fitness, the health of the three spheres, and the spiritual integration of the existing well-being of our personal lives.

Q: Will Chi Kung do the same thing?

Master Ni: T'ai Chi and Chi Kung are similar. If you separate the movements of T'ai Chi Chuan into sections or single movements, you will have Chi Kung. If you put the movements of Chi Kung together in a different sequence, it is T'ai Chi. They are each slightly different ways of practice with the same goals.

It is interesting to know that some single movements of either of the two practices can often give great benefit when done repeatedly. For example, if you have shoulder pain, you can do a certain movement constantly until the pain goes away. Then you can do something else. If someone has a breathing or other problem, Chi Kung has specific therapeutic purposes. How does it have the power to heal disease? The power does not come from outside, it comes from you. You conduct your own energy to help yourself. This is another proof of its possibility for your personal achievement. It is a spiritual power. Some highly practiced people can use this power to cure other people, but anyone can at least use the power to cure oneself. This power, one's own enhanced spiritual energy, can also change the destiny of one's life and death.

Body Secrets and Chakras

Q: In the theory of chakras in the body, I have read that the chakras, starting from the bottom, are red, orange, yellow, green in the heart, blue, violet and white in the crown. And that blue and yellow are the colors that when combined make green, which is in the heart center. That is the medium connecting both parts. Does the Integral Way have a similar theory?

Master Ni: I like your question. This comes from the yoga tradition. The yoga tradition is a kind of program. The program has divided the body into a theory of coloration. As a spiritual concept, it is effective, but unfortunately not in reality. We can use color because all colors have a different function, especially when applied to different chakras or energy points.

Physically, each chakra is a center of the nervous system. Practically, each center has a group of spirits that function there. The yogic tradition has an image, color, sound and special spiritual word for each chakra to help you communicate with the spirits of that chakra. You must understand, however, that the yogic system is a method of training, not the plain reality. Mostly this training stabilizes your nervous system or nerve energy. In the beginning it is a good tool to help the mind.

Many people reach this spiritual understanding. The Indian contribution is great; it can help people's minds and emotions. High Indian sages might also achieve immortality; but for the most part, those things cannot be learned by the public.

Anyone who has quiet time and sincerity can follow the yogic tradition's program and experience something about their chakras. You can also prove it by yourself. The achievement of physical health and spiritual stability is not a product of the external program, however. It is the result of the mind and body having reached the original naturalness that brings about direct spiritual achievement.

I do not disrespect anything. I respect the traditional experience from all the cultures. Surely, they are all our human ancestors. They worked for us and lived for all of us. Religions or traditions of the Middle East interest me too. This is especially true because I come from Asia, and in the last 2,000 years the Indian and Chinese cultures have strongly affected each other. Some Indian practices were initiated in China. Some of the Chinese religions were initiated in India, at least in terms of external layout or ritual, and so forth. I think the Indian ancestors did a great job in helping the human mind. They did not necessarily develop the mind, but they had a practice that could be used for pacifying or sedating the mind, to slow it down and separate it from any difficult, ugly or painful reality. In India, life is hard. Buddhism especially helps a person to slow down or sedate the mind rather than tonify or excite it.

Q: What is the correlation to the colors in the Integral Way?

Master Ni: Bodily energy has colors as aura. The internal energy movement from the five main viscera and the assistant organs are organized in the principle of five elements (see the beginning part of *The Book of Changes and the Unchanging Truth, Tao the Subtle Universal Law and the Integral Way of Life,* or refer to acupuncture textbooks). Internal movement is taught separately; traditionally, there is "The Movement of Five Elements" and the movement of eight natural energies (Ba Gua).

Each energy point is a center. It has a different meaning and a different spiritual level corresponding to the spiritual world. Some traditions divide the levels into seven and other traditions divide it into nine. Each physical energy checkpoint is a spiritual center. In ancient times, they were called "Heavens," so sometimes you will read that somebody refers to seven "Heavens" or nine "Heavens." Practically, the only essential practice is the one which integrates all nine Heavens. Lao Tzu says, "The high one makes the low ones as the foundation." Thus the low ones cannot be neglected, but they are not the purpose of cultivation.

We need to know the most effective way to achieve our goals. Those who have experienced different traditions and different ways of practice enjoy learning certain things or perhaps giving themselves a broad foundation. Then they come to the Integral Way, perhaps for more depth. Surely, all spiritual training can help a person do other things.

Indian spiritual practice is in a straight line with still points. In the Integral Way, the practices are in a circle; they make the front and back connect. The front movement is not as difficult as the back, because of the spinal bone. Sometimes a person's sitting position or postural habits cause some obstruction of energy movement. There are three checkpoints on the back spinal bone through which it is difficult for the energy to pass.

You have done yoga before and now you are doing a circle practice. Internal practices of the Integral Way include mainly three ways: 1) a straight line as the axis - from the top of the head to the perineum (the region between the sexual organs and the anus). This practice of internal energy movement is termed "energy movement and gathering on the central yellow path." 2) Energy circulation on the middle front and back lines is termed "the small orbit circulation." 3) Energy circulation on all the eight auxiliary energy channels is termed "the big orbit circulation," which is different from the above two. Each of the three cannot replace one other. There are other ways too.

Why does the Integral Way emphasize cyclic movement? We discovered that if the practice is only in separate and still points, each center would become stagnant. Once energy is gathered, it can move to fill other centers. The entire universe does not stop, even for a second. It is always moving, no matter how subtly; you do not even notice it. Take the example of the planets traveling in a circular orbit. We did not make the human mind our teacher; we made nature our teacher.

The *Tao Teh Ching* says that humans learn from earth. We are attached to the earth. The earth learns from Heaven and Heaven learns from nature. Nature learns from the Integral Truth; the Integral Truth is the subtle law. So the subtle law governs everything. Cyclic movement expresses the subtle law. It is not the focus of partial fact which is limited experience.

Spiritual Development Brings Different Appreciation

If any tradition can help stop the spiritual religious conflict and achieve world peace, I will be the first one to follow it. I will dedicate my life to it. Unfortunately, so far, they always express something incomplete. So let us, the new generation of all human ancestors, find a truthful way. Not according to where someone was born, but according to what does the best service and is most truthful, effective and useful.

Achieved ones use different methods. If we were all going to Paris, some would fly over there, some would take a boat and some would ride a train. You can take any way. According to my personal experience, I think that the deep level of achievement should be the same, no differences. It is not the method or the differences of travel we need to be attached to, but we can respect any truthful achievement. True achievement can be obtained by simple means, but it is also hard to reach.

When a person wants to go upward, I think an easy way to get there is to build a ladder and go step-by-step, so I am showing you how to build a ladder. It is not my own invention, but a composite of all experiences. In this moment, I wish to introduce my new friends to Gentle Movement or internal spiritual art because it is a useful tool. I do not think all my ancestors did the same thing, because they used different tools. They mostly sat in meditation. I do differently, but I wish to achieve the same purpose.

Acupuncture that is practiced according to the T'ai Chi theory sometimes uses a method called tonifying and sometimes uses a method called sedating, according to the situation. There is no one way that can be utilized all the time; sometimes you need to tonify and sometimes you need to sedate, according to the case. In a case where energy is congested in a part of the body or if a person is excited or hypertense, he needs a sedating effect. That means to slow the person down. Some people are already slow, so we need to stimulate, or to tonify, to make the people gather more energy. The same is true in natural spiritual practices at a certain level. You pay attention to what your energy is doing and then apply the proper practice to maintain yourself in perfect balance.

Religious teaching has a function. Hinduism and Buddhism contribute to the good function of sedating. If carried to an extreme, the effect is devitalization and makes people less interested in life activity. Christianity, for example, is usually more tonifying because in its conceptual structure God helps you, which also might make a person more outward. Carried to an extreme, it makes people too fervent or aggressive. The teaching of the Integral Way does not work on rigid external establishment. The natural realistic situation determines who or what needs to be tonified and who or what needs to be sedated. The Integral Way also offers different practices with different developed methods. Gentle Movement, practically, is an interplay of contraction and expansion, tonification and sedation.

For example, in the *Tao Teh Ching* there is a illustration about stretching the bow. When a bow is stretched, the lower part is raised, the higher part is lowered, the narrow part widened and the wide part narrowed. This describes the management of your life. It is subtle, so you need to develop your vision to understand that deeply.

In doing Gentle Movement or Internal Arts, you learn how to manage the three spheres of your energy: physical, mental and spiritual. Once you learn energy management, you can make the three energies connect, gather, align and attune to be in perfect harmony. Then you will experience joy inside and harmony outside, and harmony inside and joy outside, too. This is a practical, approachable method. In meditation, sometimes we tend toward fantasy and do not see the direct result. I believe that a moving meditation like Gentle Movement, if done correctly, can help you both spiritually and physically at the same time.

Some people who do yoga stay in the mountains and forests. They are respectable. They do not take anything from the world, and they also do not purposely wish to influence the world. They go to achieve themselves spiritually. They do not do it for show, income or any other social benefit. That is the difference between being spiritual and being religious, as I define it. Yet, it is also not necessary to stay in the mountains and forests to be spiritual.

The seven chakras of the yoga system are a spiritual discovery. Discovering the seven important nervous centers in the body can never be assisted by any external device. It is a respectable and valuable achievement in spiritual practice, but as to what color, word, picture or sound is traditionally associated with each chakra, there is not any kind of definite or scientific knowledge. It can be considered an association that is built up between the mind and the chakras. Using a color or word, etc., is more a kind of energy conducting rather than just experiencing a natural, plain nerve center.

In the Chinese system, chakras were discovered long ago. The ancient developed Chinese went further to discover the fourteen main energy channels and eight extra energy channels. Sometimes people call these channels meridians. Each channel or meridian has many energy points which have been found to correspond with organs, secretion systems, glandular functions, the nervous system, lymph system and immune system, and so on. This was a spiritual discovery that has become common knowledge and been put into service for healing the general public.

In ancient times, all healers were realizers of the Integral Way who had developed themselves spiritually. As I mentioned, they attained special knowledge about the body and energy points and their use. They also knew about different herbs and their use, about chi practice and many other helpful, effective healing methods. In ancient China, the purpose of medical development was not financial growth. Healing was a spiritual offering of those realizers of natural spiritual truth who gave their service for no charge. They did not ask for anything back. It was part of their external practice aside from their internal practice. The use of energy points, compared to other systems, took at least 10,000 to 20,000 more years of spiritual work.

I believe there is some difference between the results and achievements of the yoga practitioners and the shiens who followed the Integral Way. Yoga usually cannot avoid Hindu religious teachings. The immortal tradition of ancient

China, except in giving a special service, remained independent of mass religious promotion. In the internal practices of the Integral Way, the primary emphasis is placed upon the transformability of energy. It is not like an idea of chakras with a fixed location for each specific energy. The discovery of the Integral Way is that sexual energy cannot always be sexual energy and brain energy cannot always be brain energy, and both energies can be transformed and sublimated to be spiritual energy. That is an advancement over the concept or notion of fixation.

Truthfully, there are lots of secrets of high achievement. Each practice will produce a different result or achievement. One example of this is a practice such as concentrating at the midpoint between the two eyes and eyebrows. This technique has been openly discussed in my own work and in the work of the yogic tradition. As it relates to the notion of reincarnation, it can be understood as follows: when a person's physical energy is deceased, the soul will follow a certain definite spiritual channel in leaving the body. Usually a soul leaves a body according to the person's spiritual condition. Generally, if the person did not cultivate at all, the soul leaves the body from the sexual organs or from the elimination organs. In the yogic tradition, this means that in his next life, the person will have a low birth. If the soul leaves the body from any of the apertures above those mentioned, the soul will come back to human life according to the place that it exited. In Indian spiritual knowledge, leaving the body through the midpoint, the so-called mystical pass, will entitle the person to be a king or emperor of the human world in the next life.

However, in my tradition, we think this point can help a person attain one's own spiritual authority and choose a positive life. The teaching of natural spiritual truth not only talks about the formation of life, nor is it limited to internal energy practices alone. Traditionally, we use natural energy to support internal energy. The chakras can only produce what is in the body, but the source of the entire universe can be immensely supportive to one's spiritual development. Therefore, we choose to combine internal practice with natural energy such as the energy of the sun, moon and stars to achieve a free or a "flying" soul. In religious terms, those two achievements of the soul might be called the flying spiritual kings and queens. That terminology is all right, but I do not adopt such a religious approach in my teaching in order to save people from their egos. More important than the name of the type of soul is to pursue that spiritual reality. All ancient religions were inspired by the natural environment. It is a matter of how one uses natural energy.

Some ask which system, Indian or Chinese, achieves higher. To a beginner, I do not think it makes any difference. Even if a person directly learns natural spiritual truth, at the beginning he or she still touches the first level of things. About high achievement: who can teach the high achievement? Nothing can be taught until a student develops enough to know the deep truth which he or she has attained step by step and reaches a certain level in spiritual self-cultivation.

In art achievement, the use of different lines, colors, lights and techniques gives an art appreciator the knowledge that different paintings are different expressions. The shallow sphere of spiritual achievement is similar to the shallow sphere of art appreciation. To the beginning art appreciator, the best is what he or she likes; it is not the real best. To a beginner, the perfect art is what he knows; it is not necessarily the same as a higher standard.

Although spiritual achievement is similar to this, the range of spiritual achievement is as vast as the number of channels on a satellite dish. A person has a wide range to choose from. However, this is still not a complete example, because only in the beginning stage of spiritual learning and achievement can a person make a choice of his or her learning by applying his or her likings, fondness, appreciation and inclination. In deep or high spirituality, there is no fixed idea or program, but a new spiritual reality which unfolds to you. This cannot be prearranged by anyone. If a person keeps the same image of himself or herself, the same "I" or the same "you" that society gives him, then he has no spiritual achievement. Society or social culture only creates stronger egos. This is why the believers of different religions become so partial to their own group and exhibit prejudice.

In this level, I have been carefully describing different spiritual qualities. A good, promising student will never miss such important points. I believe you need to review and deeply study all the work I have produced.

The Steps to Becoming Spiritually Immortal

Q: Could you go over the steps to immortality again, please.

Master Ni: At the highest level, you do not need to do anything. You are a natural immortal. At the second level, you take your general nutrition from food, air and water and so forth to be your physical energy. Your sexual energy is the essence of your physical energy.   Then refine your sexual energy to be chi.   Chi is higher, it can also be transferred back into sexual energy, but it is more subtle. One of its functions is immunity. There are other steps to immortality. I have just briefly touched upon it. Allow me to come back to it some other time.

I would really like you to understand chi. It is hard to tell if you have it until you pay attention, so let me give a few examples.   An achieved Chinese painter who does painting or calligraphy will sit down and do an excellent piece of work on a day when his chi or energy is good. He knows it is good and he is satisfied.   Sometimes such a piece is a masterpiece or the work of a lifetime.   It is not something that just happens, of course, because he may have trained his whole life to be able to create such a masterpiece, but it is the product of his training and his personal energy. Suppose though, he did not sleep well, or he did something unusual like indulging in too much sex or drinking too much alcohol.   Even though it is the same person with the same skill and 30, 40 or 50 years of training, if he has no chi or energy, he cannot do the same refined work. This is true of sculpture or anything artistic.

Let us take an example of someone who is not an artist. A speaker of high eloquence can talk very well. It is a great talent to speak appropriately and beautifully. If we invite this person to give a lecture and his energy is damaged through drink, sex or whatever, the same person cannot produce the same effect. It is all because of the difference of the energy.

So from that, you can understand that it is chi that makes a person refined or able to create something of high quality. The same is true in everyday life; if a person's energy is low, he may have trouble driving, making good shopping decisions, etc. The chi, though subtle, is still provable, from those conditions or phenomena. It is possible to experience the subtle change within your own body, if you pay attention.

The spiritual level is a high level. I would like to give my own experience as an example. When first I came to the United States, I did not have a strong foundation in English. I had learned English from a dictionary. I read the dictionary and remembered the words, but I used Chinese sentence structure. Because the demand from my students was so great soon after I arrived here, I started to teach a class on the *I Ching*. Please be assured that teaching the *I Ching* is no small task. Not only are the concepts difficult in any language, but it also takes great vocabulary and language skill to communicate this to others. Because of my busy medical practice, I had no time to prepare beforehand for the class by referring to the dictionary or writing out the right words in a good combination to be able to teach. I more or less had to teach without preparation. There is one benefit to no advance preparation, and that is no preconception. My way of being able to accomplish each class successfully with no preparation was by meditating or resting for a half hour or an hour to gather my spiritual energy before giving the class. So I prepared for the class by nurturing my energy rather than reading a grammar book. Once I was in the class, the words just flowed.

If I did not do this process of gathering energy, it would have been different. The lectures I gave were going to be made into a book, and on some chapters I myself did not think I did a good job. So in those cases, I taught the class twice, also to make sure that everybody understood.

Lecturing and writing are two different energies. To lecture, I always need to nurture my energy to supplement my limited English. I think that not everybody understood everything that I said. However, it was not only my language they came to hear. Mostly, they understood through reading my energy and correlating it with the words. So they felt good and perhaps attained an even better understanding than they would have if I were an eloquent speaker. Understanding on an energy level will often take a person farther than words alone.

This is how I communicate with my students. What can you call that? Some might call it charisma, but I have no name for it. Mostly, it is my chi. Or because my level is usually higher, it is my sen, spiritual energy, that communicates with my students, especially those who are aware.

The energy that is used in talking, writing, artistic expression, performing, office work, housework, etc., is chi. Once I gather all this chi and refine it, it becomes my spirit, my spiritual being. It is the beingness of spirit; it is sen. This is more profound.

Yet I would like you to understand that nurturing chi is very important. You will experience that on some occasions you react smoothly to things; you think your performance is beautiful, and it is satisfying to you. Sometimes you may not feel you do well. Only if your energy is good will you do well. You do not need to check out other people, you only need to check out yourself to find out if you will be successful in a show or not.

Even in handling business affairs, the practice is the same. Basically, there is no secret; or you could say that the secret is sincerity. Only with sincerity can you gather energy and lay the foundation. Only with sincerity can you develop the high skill for whatever your goal is. Once you put your mind to be there, you find your strength and support, because it is your spirit leadership that is there.

Chapter 5

The Integral Truth
Is the Unity of All Differences

Master Kou Hong and other great masters inspired me to dedicate myself to working toward a healthy and naturally orderly world. The following discussions are the contribution of spiritual individuals of different generations. All were enlightened by the Integral Way and found their application in various situations of life. These visions are the treasures of all humankind in finding true spiritual development in life.

I
What is the Integral Way or Integral Truth?

When our early spiritually developed ancestors observed the nature of their external surroundings and the internal landscape of their lives, they found that no single fact or truth could be sorted out as single existent phenomenon. In other words, the whole truth of the universe cannot be contained in a simple example or a statement which the human mind can grasp, because the truth of the universe itself is a unique species, specimen or sample. The truth of the universe constantly manifests in different forms. For example, when human people describe something, they say it is red, blue or another color, or all colors. However, once you describe a thing as having all colors, you cannot say it has no color. Practically, there is no "no color." Color is produced by different effects of light. You can describe a thing as either tall or short, but you cannot describe a thing as being both tall or short. The concepts of tall or short are established by a common standard of two or more samples, yet the reality of all things exists beyond any standard. The existence of these things is not decided by any standard.

The integral truth of the universe, or the integral universe, was observed by the ancient wise ones who found that the truth of the universe is that things live as themselves. This is true at all times in all places. It was out of the intuitive capability of the ancient wise ones or the universal mind itself that the word "Way" was used to describe the integral truth. As a student of human life millions of years later, I try to illustrate the mystical word "Way" that cannot be a human invention. "Way" is the ultimate spiritual truth that all things are interrelated. It is a great self discovery by humans themselves. The Integral Way becomes the spiritual development of universal mind itself. When the intelligence of the human mind connects with the universal mind, it reflects differently than a mind that is unconnected. Therefore, the trustworthy approach in moving toward the Integral Truth is to work to develop the human mind in order to reach the universal mind or universal spirit, which is the integral spirit of the universe.

In many past generations, individuals at different levels of spiritual development came to an understanding of the Integral Truth. Integral Truth can be thought of as the universal law that can be applied to each human individual, the world or anything. Because the spiritual development of each individual is different, and even people who have the same spiritual development have a different focus, the expression of the Integral Truth is different too. In different nations and races, because of the social backgrounds and limitations of the teachers and leaders, spiritual develop- ment also expresses differences.

The Integral Truth is recognized by different times and different individuals and is expressed differently. The fact that the Integral Truth has been realized and communicated by individuals with different frames of reference can help us align ourselves in the subtle law. This assists our under- standing, so that we can achieve it in order to help us to accomplish our lives perfectly. The following was the illustration of different people at a different time in the Chinese region.

The first meaning of the word Tao, or the Integral Truth, is a way or path, a route.

The second meaning of the Integral Truth is the origin or the substance of all things.

The third meaning of the word Integral Truth is one- ness, or unity. Why is Truth oneness? It is oneness because it is energy, the universal prime energy. The prime energy exists in all things, places and times, and is never separated or divided from itself. Therefore, the Natural Subtle Truth is one. If Truth is one, who else is there to know Truth?

There are levels of existence. On the absolute level, the Universal Subtle Truth is one. On the relative sphere, the inquisitive nature of the human mind limits itself and keeps itself from knowing Universal Truth unless a breakthrough is found.

The fourth meaning is nothingness. It means no partiality. It does not mean nothingness at an absolute level, but nothingness at the relative level. It is a limitation of the human mind that when we discuss or express something, it must fall into a relative or dualistic pattern. The Subtle Truth is nothingness, or nothing that can be described on the relative level in which the language or conceptual mind can exercise its capability.

Further, the Ultimate Spiritual Truth is nothingness. Nothingness makes you unattached to secondary creation as triviality and partiality. With nothingness, you embrace the potence of the universe, the potence of nature. If you think about something, it means you are linked with something. But the Natural Subtle Truth is nothingness before it becomes something. The Subtle Truth is the origin of all. When you think about nothing, you relate with the universal subtle origin before it is formed to be anything. Thus, the Universal Truth can be reached by being natural and keeping an empty mind.

When you talk on the telephone, your mind is already occupied by the thought of things and people. When you hang up, your mind becomes natural. When your mind is occupied, you disrupt the connection between yourself and the spirits. You cannot hear them. When you become neutral, you can quietly listen to all the voices. To be empty minded is to become open to listening to real communication. When you become very quiet, you can listen to all the voices. This is the way to reach the high sensitive spiritual energy or God. By practicing quietude, you can be highly spiritually developed, attain immortality and live an eternal life with the Integral Truth.

The fifth meaning of the term Subtle Integral Truth is law. The Integral Truth is T'ai Chi, the ultimate law.

The sixth meaning of the term Integral Truth is mind. On the surface of the mind, there are many manifestations. Yet when you reach the depth of mind, you will find that the mind is just a piece of energy. This energy communicates with the energy of all things, so because the Subtle Truth is energy, it is the mind in human people.

The seventh meaning is energy. Energy means transformation. Energy is always proceeding from something to become something else; this defines transformation. This transformable energy follows certain laws or pathways.

One of the predictable patterns or laws of energy transformation is the subtle law, which is also called the law of yin and yang. Yin and yang are the expression of the Integral Truth. The division between yin and yang is caused by the transformation of the universal primal energy, which is also called chi, into two different manifestations.

The eighth meaning of the Integral Truth is human rule or the way of humanity. Righteousness, freedom, equality and universal love all express the Universal Subtle Law.

The Universal Spiritual Truth is the origin or substance of the universe and of everything. It cannot be reached by sensory function. It is transcendent. It is behind the phenomena of nature and society. It is the origin of all things and the universe. The Integral Truth is the original fundamental nature of the entire universe.

All things have internal or fundamental elements. These internal elements exist deeply in all things. The internal communication that occurs subtly between all things expresses the unity, the commonality and oneness of the universe. This is what the Integral Truth is about.

The original nature of the universe is not dead, it is alive. Therefore there is movement and activity. This activity, movement and motion follow certain laws. When certain laws are applied, a given situation will become productive; otherwise, it will be destructive. The law that maintains the good condition of existing things is the Integral Truth. The Integral Subtle Truth is the procession of change which occurs when a thing exists or moves. It is an orderly, predictable pattern of change. Therefore, the Integral Truth includes all things and is everywhere. There is nothing outside of it, because the Integral Truth is the biggest. There is nothing inside of it, because the Integral Truth is the smallest. The Subtle Integral Truth itself contains yin and yang; something and nothing, one and two, moving or stillness, law or energy.

The Integral Truth is neither spiritual nor material; it is the unification of the two. Thus, the Integral Way is the apparent unification between a confrontation or a conflict. This unification can be seen in the evolution of the universe or human society. That is the Subtle Spiritual Truth. In a general sense, the Subtle Integral Truth can also be considered to be the principle behind politics, morality or the social code of normal human society.

In different generations, most people understood that the Integral Truth is the Way, law or proper method of living which can assist people's lives and help them maintain a good natural condition. Then, people also understood that the Universal Subtle Truth is the way to unify Heaven and people. Heaven and people are not separated. The communication, connection and transportation between Heaven and humans is the Integral Way.

The Subtle Truth is energy. Energy responds to energy of similar wavelength or frequency, so the unification and communication among all the differences occurs energetically. Despite differences between the things, there is an internal communication system. I hope this helps us to understand that the Subtle Truth is the energy that enlivens living people. The Subtle Spiritual Truth is the creative generator.

Beyond language and conceptual structure is the Integral Truth. The Integral Truth is the power of harmony, which is the power of unification of all differences.

The Integral Truth is energy, not something already entrapped in any form. Before something is formed, it exists in freedom. After something is formed, the universal energy is entrapped, limited and defined by form and its capacity. Only when the form is dissolved is there a return to freedom or achieving freedom without allowing the form to be the obstacle. That is unless, of course, one learns to attain the Ultimate Subtle Truth while still in the bodily form.

The Integral Truth is the reason why we have Heaven, why we have universe, why we have life, why we have this and why we have that. There is a common reason for all existence and non-existence. The one who aligns oneself with the Integral Way has a good existing condition. The things that are not aligned with the universal law seem to defeat themselves and cannot sustain themselves in a good existing condition.

II
The Integral Truth and Mind

Now we will continue to talk about the fact that we have a mind and a heart. Sometimes the heart and mind are in conflict with each other: a person's emotion says that one thing needs to be done, and the mind says that a different thing needs to be done. When the heart and mind harmonize, this is the Integral Way. The transportation, communication and harmony between the heart and mind is the Integral Truth. You do not need to go far to look for God.

When you do anything, bring your heart and mind together in agreement first. Mind is the sphere of intellect, knowledge and experience. Heart is the sphere of high conscience and sympathy. When your heart is accepted by your mind, your mind likes to work to accomplish the heart's wishes but in such a circumstance, one should not let the mind itself be carried away by the external situation. Because natural morality presides in the human heart it takes care of the formed life's natural morality. Also, when it gets along with other formed lives, it extends natural morality and natural virtue to them unless the mind brings about external conflict by its knowledge. This means natural morality presides in the human heart. A person of humanistic heart and natural morality applies one's morality in one's own life. Such a person also extends this natural morality or natural virtue to other people or natural lives, unless the wisdom or knowledge of the mind tells it to do otherwise. In this last case of disharmony between the heart and mind, the person probably ignores the heart.

We know that the integral spiritual truth is energy. Using your own mind, you can guide energy to do anything, but mind is energy itself. The mind is a powerful energy. It can guide a person's physical and spiritual energy to do many things. Nevertheless, much of the time, one's spiritual or physical energy knows what to do without the mind. In other words, sometimes the mind interferes and blocks what is natural. Sometimes, in fact, the mind will tell the energy to move in a way that is not best for the person. Energy knows by itself which direction to move in without being directed by the mind. If you move in a certain direction, your energy will increase, whereas in another direction, it will decrease. I am talking about subtle energy here.

If you put a young man and young woman in a room, their energy knows how or where to move, but in that situation the mind of knowledge and the heart of moral conscience must also do something. Because human life is developed, it is not totally physical energy. If you move in a certain direction, you are against the subtle law, and hasten your own self-destruction. The Integral Truth is the universal subtle energy and is therefore its own law, thus it is universal subtle law. The Integral Truth is not an idea, but the reality of the universe.

Humans have what is called a humanistic nature, and this humanistic nature, correctly fulfilled, is the Integral Truth.

In spiritual self-cultivation, a certain alignment needs to be made. The alignment is like putting yourself on the right side of the freeway and driving your car without worry. The division between the directions of traffic flow make you know that you are safe. Driving on the right side of the freeway is meeting the Integral Way.

The Subtle Integral Truth is everywhere. The Integral Truth can be universal and it can be in the human sphere. The Integral Truth is within your universal self, because you are part of the one life of the universe.

The Natural Subtle Truth is known by people who have grown their own spiritual self-awareness. They become aware of their own spirit. They know that the substance of life and the substance of the universe is one and the same.

In other words, the substance of life is the branches growing out of the substance of the universe, the trunk.

If the universe was created, spirit must have existed before the world happened. If the world is natural development, there is still spiritual energy coming from the universal development of the entirety of the universe.

I hope this helps explain the point of connection between scientific and religious theories of how the universe was created. One theory states the universe was created by God and the other states that the universe evolved naturally. Both are true. If the universe was created, the creator had no experience at the beginning; that unexperienced spirit is the original universal energy. That energy can be considered the subtle universal origin or the Integral Truth. After creation, there must have been further development of what was originally created, kind of like a supplement. It means creation was a supplement made through development, or development happened after the creation.

We live in the world. Human life is a company of lives. There were many lives before human life came into the world, such as plant and animal life.

Who is the master or ruler of the universe? In one sense, all lives are on the same level of equality. Each life carries the universal nature within itself and is looking for better expression and improvement in its own life. It wishes to realize its self nature in a better way. Still, inside and outside, the life is a unified mastery. That mastery only expresses a subtle universal law which governs all beings, all lives and all things. That is the Integral Truth. That is the subtle law. That is the subtle energy.

III
The Integral Truth and Ethics

If ethics come from the growth of spiritual self-awareness, then one could say that ethics come from the Integral Truth. According to the situation and different levels of development of spiritual reality, different customs were created. There are reasonable and unreasonable customs. There is useful social order, and there is useless social restraint. Anything that follows the order of harmony, the normalcy of the universe and the normalcy of a productive, creative, healthy life is the expression of the natural subtle truth. The depth of ethics is to do nothing extra, desire nothing extra, and tame the scatteredness of curiosity.

We have mentioned that the ultimate spiritual truth is the masterly energy of the universe. Sometimes we call it Heaven or Tien. Tien is the expression of the spiritual truth. It expresses authority over all lives because Heaven or Tien is subtle energy. Unfortunately, people have a rigid idea about Heaven or Tien that is not truthful. It is not Heaven that causes them problems, it is their idea about what Heaven is that causes trouble. The idea about Heaven formed by humans expresses something like injustice and unrighteousness. Does the masterly energy or Heaven reward the good and punish the bad? Yes.

Because the Integral Truth is energy, it stretches to all lives and all existence. In the sense of human people, if a person overextends or pulls oneself by the mind into many different directions, then destruction or self-extinction will happen. That is the punishment, while circumventing or preventing future trouble from occurring is the reward.

We already discussed that the subtle energy is the origin behind all phenomena. Are substance and phenomenon two different things? No, they are not. Allow me to give an example. On the land, everything that exists and is displayed in front of our eyes is the phenomena of life. In the sky, the phenomena are the clouds, sky, stars, sun and moon. On the land, the substance is life energy. In the sky, the substance is the source of all energy, material and higher potency. Now let me ask again: Are the substance and the phenomenon of individual existence two things or one? If they are one thing, why do they have a different expression? What is the unified communication between them? They are one thing that expresses itself differently due to circumstance, and the connection between them is the subtle energy. No substance exists apart from the phenomenon. Phenomenon is unified with substance; it directly expresses the existence of the substance of the universe in the deep sphere. So the Integral Truth is the unification between the individual existence of phenomenon and substance of all existence.

IV
The Integral Way and the Subtle Law

Through the spiritual development of the ancient sages, the Integral Truth basically is the Way or the road. By their illustration, the Integral Way carries at least five meanings.

First, the Integral Way must have a definite direction. The Integral Truth expresses a direction or tendency which follows a certain law or rhythm. This law is knowable. Thus, you can understand the change that occurs in things, because the direction of its movement and change always follow the law.

Second, the Integral Way must be straight. It cannot be twisted or confused. If it is twisted, you cannot reach the destination, or you will misguide people. This meaning might lead you to believe that the Integral Way is a principle that everybody or everything must follow. That is correct.

Third, the Subtle Integral Way means the connection between the starting point and the destination. Between the starting and ending points is a certain distance. That distance is called the process. Therefore, the Integral Way means the process of change and movement in all things.

Fourth, the Integral Way must express no obstruction. There is no obstruction that the Integral Truth cannot go through. The meaning of the human world was established by the guidance of the Integral Way.

Fifth, the Integral Way is a guide, guidepost or road sign that leads people to work in a certain direction.

The original five meanings were grasped by ancient people's intuitive mind directly from the Integral Way. Different understanding came from the intellectual minds of later people. When the Integral Truth is applied to the subtle universal law, subtle universal energy or universal prime energy, these five functions express the meaning of the Integral Truth.

V
The Integral Way and Harmonious Order

In ancient times, the word "Tao" was widely used to describe the Integral Truth. Sometimes Tao or Integral Truth is used to describe the rule or protection of the subtle sphere, or the destiny of a good government. In ancient times, the establishment of political power or a government received the support of people, so there was no struggle over accepting a particular government or a power as the center of society; it was just naturally recognized by the people. This gave people the idea that the establishment of a good government was the Heavenly law or way of Heaven. Thus they believed that Heaven gave its support by either allowing or empowering a new king or new social leader. This is one concept about the Integral Truth that people held in ancient times.

How then should a government behave politically to stay in accord with the Integral Truth? How can it best help or govern society? It must have principles, direction, regulation or law and so forth. In ancient times, laws were decided by the political center. That type of direction was called the "Way of the King." It was also called the "Law over the Kings."

You know, even in ancient society, there was trouble. Some people are simply more aggressive and cause suffering to others, thus it became necessary to have social regulation, or law, to determine the punishment of aggressive people. In ancient times, this was also recognized as the Integral Truth because a society or nation needs lasting peace, security, sufficiency and correct administration. All of this was included in the meaning of the Integral Truth.

There are different kinds of relationship among people. One kind is a horizontal relationship among equals, and another is a vertical relationship between government officials and the people. Among people, some need help and some would like to give help. In China, giving help also had the connotation of the Integral Way. The Way has the meaning of help, the way of help or practical help.

Sometimes people need to express themselves by making a statement that expresses a personal idea or makes a comment. When an idea was expressed clearly in the ancient language, that way of speaking was also called the Integral Truth.

In ancient times, developed people trusted that behind the world was a master, but the master could not be seen. They believed that the master was the subtle law. Sometimes the subtle law was called the law of Heaven.

The law of Heaven was also expressed by the movement or rotation of Heavenly bodies. From observation of cyclic movement, the ancients discovered one objective law: that all things begin to develop and then reach their full growth and prosperity. If they did not take care, however, they would always go into a downward cycle and disappear. This recognition became an objective law. Therefore, they postulated that moderation and humility within prosperity was more important at the time of full growth than at the beginning, when development is still weak.

About social relationships, after generations, a natural law or code developed which all people obeyed. A social mode or social code arose which reinforced that if a person did a certain thing, other people would agree, but if a person did certain other things, people would not agree. There is a range of behavior that people think is correct, and beyond that range is incorrect. Thus, the way to handle different relationships, such as natural, blood, social, business and all other kinds of relationships developed subtly without any language or particular rules written down. This is the way of humankind. It presents the harmonious relationship between the way of Heaven and the way of humans.

In ancient times, people thought that the influence of Heaven was far away and that the influence of people was close at hand. They believed that the harmony between the way of Heaven and the way of people provided long lasting blessings with the agreement and support of all people. At least, they knew this was true until a society became corrupt. If there is conflict between Heaven and people, or if the leadership of a society is against the Integral Truth as the Subtle Law - although the conflict only appeared in some area or for a short time - they knew that the good time would soon be over. That was the first thought.

A second thought was that the law of Heaven is not partial, but they also noticed that Heaven helps the one with virtue and supports the one with good ethics. Such an individual is usually helpful not only to his own family and relatives, but to all people. This made them understand that the Integral Truth as the Subtle Law is the sense of justice, righteousness and public spirit. They accepted this as a new meaning of the Integral Way.

The Integral Way is not intellectual learning. The Integral Truth can be known by people's own spiritual self-awareness. When people came to the stage where they knew the difference between themselves and other animals, humanistic attitudes began to develop. In that stage, the sages focused on how humans were different from other animals, which began to bring about humanistic attitudes. Humanism was produced from internal spiritual self-awareness; the sages decided the Integral Way was humanistic.

VI
The Integral Truth and Human Society

In ancient society, there was no social regulation or code known as law, but people slowly developed a proper approach to accept or handle other people. The result was the development of a suitable social code or mode. Another way to describe this is manners or custom. Discipline in doing what was right came from oneself, out of the consideration which is the mark of individual spiritual self-awareness. Individuals recognized that there were differences between how they and other people behaved. Communication or the connection between people, the common way of socializing, is called the Integral Way.

At the beginning, when the Integral Truth was applied to human society, people focused upon five things. First, respect and help was offered to older, weaker or younger people. Second, one was loyal to one's own life. Third, one maintained a helpful attitude toward others and forgave those who caused offense. Fourth, faithfulness and trustworthiness were respected. Ancient society was not a society of written contracts, but a society in which people were recognized by faithfulness and honesty in their own words and behavior. To make one's words and behavior accepted as strongly as cash comes from the practice of faithfulness and trustworthiness. Fifth, maintaining balance was considered a noble virtue. It means not doing anything to excess.

These five things are the cardinal virtues of a natural personality or the natural signature of human spiritual development. This learning or awareness occurred in the first stage of development, because no development other than the natural important virtues had occurred.

At this time, no government was established. Governments were established after the human population grew, society formed and conflict between people was aggravated. Once society moved to tackle the conflicts, there was need to establish a center of society. Thus, government slowly appeared for the purpose of taking care of people's needs. One or more people were recognized as leaders. This person or people continued to lead a group to exercise their helpfulness and offer service to people. That is called humanistic politics or humanistic administration, and was very valued in ancient times. It is called the Integral Way.

VII
The Integral Truth and Progress

There are two types of capability in human knowledge. One type is intellectual and depends upon external learning. This is the kind of learning you get in school. Spiritual self-awareness is a different type of learning. It takes a long time for a person to experience many different environments with different types of stimulation. Then, if you are the right person, your spiritual self-awareness will grow.

If an environment has the same type of people living in it, some of them will grow their spiritual self-awareness and others will not. Knowledge of the Integral Truth, knowing the existence of the subtle truth or subtle energy, is spiritual self-awareness, not an external pursuit.

After human life was formed, people lived in darkness for millions of years. Some of them slowly developed spiritual awareness. Unfortunately, that self-awareness was not the kind of intellectual knowledge that could be passed down to anyone else. Spiritual development can only be carried by the immortal soul. Through different types of reincarnation, such development can either be maintained and continued or lost because of life circumstances.

Some of the external traits of people's spiritual development were recognized as good examples and were described orally or in writing which became good spiritual education and was kept to be taught to other people to help the growth of their spiritual self-awareness. This is the natural process of an individual's developing spiritual self-awareness. It can be kindled and inspired, but different opportunities bring about different development.

People lived on earth for a long time. Slowly, they attained awareness of simple matters like the alternation of day and night and the four seasons. These things did not come to their notice until their spiritual growth began. It may sound unusual that it took people such a long time to notice the alternation of day and night, but many things were taken for granted and given no meaning. Those external factors were continually presented to them until a certain capability of recognition was attained through the growth of spiritual self-awareness. Therefore, the Integral Truth became the path, become the way, of alternation and the harmony between two different energies such as light and dark, hot and cold. In short, when the ancients became aware of such things, they considered them as the Integral Way. The Integral Way became the path of alternation, cycling or harmony between any two different energies.

After that, ancient people developed still further. They learned to distinguish subtle reality from existing living phenomena, life materials, etc. They became aware that all things went through the four stages of birth, growth, decline and death. They also recognized that everything contained natural primal energy. They began to wonder, before the birth of a thing, of a life, where was the energy? After the extinction of the thing or the life, where does the energy go? And what is the common connection between all things that present themselves? Thus, at this stage, the self-awareness and capability of human people was to know that there are two levels to life. One level is formed life, and the other level is unformed. Surely, the universal primal energy was formable, but the formable world was very limited. The ancients became aware that there was a huge, enormous, tremendous reality of universal primal energy that was not formed. It was everywhere; it existed above the formed. What is above the formed is called the Integral Truth. What is formed is called "things."

Then the ancient people further concluded that it was possible that an ultimate law existed. They believed that the ultimate law was the generating power of the universe; the ability of the universe to continue generating itself. The expression of continual generation was that first there was one; from one came two, yin and yang. From two came four, because each yin or yang energy continued to give birth to yin and yang. This continued to become eight types of energy, then things continued to develop further, with no end. But to control the multiple world there is the deepest law, which is the simple reality as the simple essence itself. The ultimate law is basically two elements, yin and yang. This is called T'ai Chi.

During that time, human self-awareness came to possess the capability of knowing internal from external and external from internal. Internal and external development are unified with the ultimate law.

At the same time, the ancients came to notice the constancy of natural cycles. The recognition of the sizes and depths of the universe, of people or of different stages is as big and deep as the intellectual range that people's mind can reach. However, with their spiritual awareness, they knew that the universe was a big piece of energy which impressed them as an alternating, cyclic, generating force. They recognized that the universe itself is a generating force, but also came to know the constancy of a subtle law behind all types of universal movement. That something is un-nameable. They decided to call that something that ex-presses constancy "Tao," or "The Integral Truth."

It means they developed the spiritual awareness to know that the universe itself was a generating force, with cyclic alternation. They also came to know that there was constancy behind the alternation, and they called it the

Integral Truth. They saw the constancy in the alternation, cycles, generation and multiplication.

Sometimes in my teaching I use the term normalcy to express the path, way, the Integral Truth or Heaven.

The ancients understood that this thing called the Integral Truth was eternal. It did not exist within the changes of human society of good and bad, but was apart from the human world. It kept moving in the same, constant law.

The ancients used their internal spiritual awareness to understand that there were different laws. Heaven has its law, earth has its law, and people have their law. Therefore, the difference between the Heavenly Way, earthly Way and human Way became known to them. One must follow such a way to bring about health and normalcy in life.

What is the Heavenly Way, earthly Way and human Way? The Heavenly Way conforms one's behavior to the highest standards because of one's high spiritual quality. In the earthly Way, one lives according to one's instincts and desires, which is considered quite low. The human Way is a moderate way of living. Surely there are people who follow their own aggressive, inconsiderate egos and attempt to triumph over the cooperative way of earth and open spiritual way of Heaven. There is a necessity for harmony between the three ways. The growing spiritual awareness of some ancients brought them to correct their habitual tendency toward competition. Modern spiritually achieved ones do the same. A certain amount of competition may still be allowed to bring about a good result from life or life activity.

The ancients observed that if a person does something against nature's cyclic movement, against alternation and so forth, harm will come. Therefore, the conception of the Integral Truth as the subtle law began to form. Although it was not written, it was understood that certain things should not be done because they would harm the life. When unity existed between the Heavenly Way, earthly Way and human Way, harmony existed along with prosperity, smoothness, joy, happiness, all good conditions and a good foundation. If there was disharmony among the three, each one had the power to bring about trouble. So the existence of the Integral Truth became stronger and more noticeable to all the people who gradually developed their spiritual self-awareness.

VIII
Integral Truth Presents Itself
in all Good Relationships

The early stages of thought about the Integral Truth came about slowly as a result of the growth of internal spiritual energy. The Integral Truth is a law. All movements, even subtle movements like thoughts, need to follow the law or trouble will happen. By recognizing the subtle law, the human race came to its first stage of maturity.

The sages in this stage decided that the Integral Truth seemed to hold mastery over all things. Yet because the Integral Truth itself has no form, the Integral Truth cannot be classified as life or as not-life. It is not in the same category of all things which exist on a competitive level. The Integral Truth is above all things. It is not a forceful strength; the reality is that masterly energy embraces all.

What is the function of the Natural, Subtle Truth? The function of the Subtle Truth is reflection or reflective movement. Anything that needs to go, must go. Anything that needs to go forward, goes forward. Anything that needs to go backward must go backward. The Subtle Truth works its subtle function among all different types of movement.

As we discussed, one type of movement is cyclic. Anything that goes to the end starts over again. The second type of movement is transfer. "A" can change to be "B," and "B" can change to be "A." Yang can transfer to be yin, and yin can transfer to be yang. So hardness and softness, honor and disgrace, victory and failure, defeat and progress, strength and weakness and so forth can all easily change into their opposites. If one side exists, the other side always exists, too.

Where there is the Heavenly Way, earthly Way and human Way, you do not need to do anything. If you do anything, it is extra activity; it is aside, extra, to the nature of the Subtle Truth. When you do nothing, remain in the neutral position and stay on the right path, there is no extra thing to be done. Then everything is smooth and stays on a natural course, following the Subtle Truth.

On the other hand, if on the human level you wish to satisfy your personal self-interest and you struggle to do something from wrong intent, such as fight to rule a country, state or company, your ambition would cause you trouble. It is better in all human affairs to follow the course of nature.

You might think the Subtle Truth is a principle, but the Subtle Truth is also nature itself. The Subtle Truth realizes itself by virtue, "Teh" or natural virtue. Natural virtue is the highest goal of self-cultivation or spiritual cultivation. It is the return to natural purity and thus to natural spiritual originalness. On the human level, it means giving up competition and contention and taking the disfavored position, accepting what is left for you. It also means retreating when you accomplish a big job or anything. Virtue or Teh is how all things can be accomplished without conflict and in accordance with the Subtle Truth. Teh describes the ability to go beyond any conflict that exists.

Teh is the realization of the Subtle Truth. In other words, the Subtle Truth is universal, but when it is applied to a specific situation, it is Teh. The Subtle Truth itself has its own attributes, such as being intangible, being reality but also being subtle essence. It is not observable by the sense organs, but it can be reached through spiritual images or spiritual development.

The Subtle Truth itself is independent but it moves unceasingly and inexhaustibly. We need to find the Subtle, Integral Way in all relationships; then the Subtle Truth can be known by us. It can be found in the relationship between the manifest and the unmanifest spheres of the universe, the somethingness and the nothingness, and so forth. The Integral Way is the unity or unification between nothingness and somethingness, existence and nonexistence, manifestation and non-manifestation.

The Ultimate Spiritual Truth is much more profound than God or spirits. For a long time, people have personified God in the image of a man. They represent God as having the same emotions and needs of people, such as the need to be pleased. However, the Ultimate Spiritual Truth is still deeper existence. Thus, the Ultimate Spiritual Truth is behind the creation of mind. A personified god is a god that needs to be pleased, a god that can make bargains.

While humans are in the process of growing, especially in the Chinese region, they hold a belief in God for a long time. There is God, but God is not personified as ordinary people imagine God to be. To the ancient Chinese, God was accepted as the common ethical rules, but they did not call it God, they called it Tao. Now we call it the Integral Spiritual Truth.

After spiritual development, the ancient people knew the reality of the universal subtle law. The universal subtle law is the subtle energy itself; it is not a separate thing. This discovery made a personified god less important. A personified God was not denied, but the concept was totally different. Discovering the subtle law was progress in having a conception of the Integral Truth.

Because the Integral Truth is universal, it cannot be argued with, bargained with or pleased. The Integral Truth is not a personified God, because all lives are equal to the life of the Integral Truth. This was progress.

The Integral Truth is recognized as the masterly energy of the world and of the universe. It is not the establishment of rulership in the human world, but the world within the world, also the world above the world.

Sometimes we use the words nature, non-extra doing, or Teh to describe the characteristics of the Integral Truth. Centeredness is another word that we use sometimes. These are the fundamental attributes of the Subtle, Integral Truth. Sometimes I use the word "virtue" to explain Teh. Teh is the communication or connection of individual life being with the Subtle Truth itself. It is in a category above or behind everything, but at the same time, it keeps forming in all lives. The healthy and normal nature of all things is called Teh. It is more recognizable than the Subtle Truth, which is behind and above and beneath all.

Chapter 6

The Integral Way Is the Unity
of Worldly Life and Spiritual Life

Master Kou Hong's contribution is not just a collection of ancient practices, but is also a compass that points the direction toward a healthy world. Through his inspiration, the following work is what I have gleaned from the discussion of different generations about what the spiritual truth is. The spiritual truth reveals itself to individuals when they attain their growth as the essence of achievement of spiritual culture. It is practical as life guidance and profound as a spiritual pursuit.

1. When the Integral Way Prevails in Practical Life

When the Integral Way is applied to practical life, it is utility. Utility means making suitable use of all things. In that way, all things make their contribution to human life. This is one way to follow the Integral Truth in practical life.

Applying the Integral Way to practical life is effectiveness. Effectiveness means accommodating the external, objective situation in achieving one's goals. At the same time one accommodates the environment, one should fully exercise the subjective functions of capability and effort. This means, do not neglect objective useful conditions, but still make the painstaking effort to accomplish what needs to be accomplished. This is called the union of Heavenly law (the Subtle Law) and individual force.

2. When the Integral Way Prevails in Life

When spiritual truth - the universal path - is in the process of producing and giving birth to life, it also continues to exist among all lives. Because spiritual energy is the substance that composes the universe, things and people, everything follows the subtle spiritual law, whether in motion, stillness or change. Spiritual reality nurtures all lives. It helps the growth of all lives. It provides for the natural growth of all lives.

The nurturing that brings growth to plants, animals, people and creative endeavors, is Teh - the universal vitality. Because of Teh, everything receives life. When we apply Teh in our daily lives, in practical ways such as organizing or managing our money, belongings, business affairs or relationships we appear to follow certain principles. These principles help bring success to what we do. We may not even be aware that we follow them.

One example of such a principle is not to waste energy. Do not waste people's energy or waste our own energy. It is good to be calm and quiet and do nothing extra. In other words, not to waste energy is to work effectively. Do not harbor any illusions or hold onto wishful thinking about not having to work hard in your life.

Another example of such a principle is, when working with others, do not be angry or display power. In your work, try to maintain a good and constructive process and embrace oneness. Embracing Spiritual Truth and respecting Teh is done by being calm and doing nothing extra. Following this is how people can live long. This is how to enjoy peace inside yourself and in the world. When following the Integral Way, things are in the right order. However, if things move against the Integral Way, then they engender a kind of internal self-confrontation. They will become lost because they lost their Integralness or Integrity.

Each of us is an individual life, a true being of the universe. Each of us was directly born through the ultimate subtle law. The way to reach the subtle truth or the Integral Way is to learn to forget the self, forget your form, forget your profit and forget your mind. If you can achieve forgetting your form, profit and mind, the sights that reach your eyes and the sounds that reach your ears will no longer please or repulse the senses, and you will not become attached to them. When your mind does not stretch out to anything, you achieve the freedom to be everywhere in the universe.

It is by the achievement of energy that people can unite and become one with the subtle origin. If you are limited by the formed life and by the pursuit of merit and profit, and if you depend upon your intelligence rather than your own intuition to help you distinguish what is right and wrong, then you cannot unite with the subtle spiritual origin.

Human life is energy. When different energies converge, a life exists. When the different energies disperse, then there is death. Human life receives its birth from the subtle origin. Also, if it is not controlled or entrapped by the physical form, the energy can return to the freedom and completeness of the subtle spiritual origin.

People with spiritual self-awareness can reach a range of depth or completeness. They can come to be united in perfection with the subtle truth and with Teh. Teh is simply harmony. It is the condition of harmony you reach after you gain the subtle truth. Therefore, humans can unite their lives with the spirit of earth and Heaven. They can unite with universal spirit and fulfill their desire for absolute spiritual freedom.

Human spiritual self-awareness develops slowly. It takes a million years for human life to evolve a little bit. It has taken millions of years for humans to have a mind with both functions: subjectivity and objectivity. A person who has cultivated spiritual awareness, caution, concentration and sincerity will know the importance of their own growth.

3. When the Integral Way Prevails in Rightful Survival

The Integral Way is rightful survival. For survival, sometimes a person cannot avoid conflict and battle, so in the human world, the fact of war cannot be stopped or changed. However, we can lessen and shorten it where possible. Unless it is absolutely necessary, the means of survival should not brought about by killing.

It is spiritual law that the person who enjoys using force will be destroyed by force. Also, it is spiritual law that a leader who can be trusted by people will gather more power. This means the leader who handles power without using force will gather more power.

We said that defending and protecting one's life is the Integral Way. Only when it is absolutely necessary, such as to protect one's natural life or for survival, should one wage war.

4. When The Integral Way Prevails in Politics

The Integral Way can also extend to politics. In general, people think that politics and spiritual learning are two different paths. That is incorrect. To participate in politics is to have responsibility for public affairs. Political leaders as well as workers in public service have a big responsibility. Anyone who is involved with the public must be objective, calm and quiet so that they can maintain a state of alertness and awareness to the conditions surrounding them. Because they influence other people, they must keep themselves open to high moral motivations and inspiration. People who maintain high morality will not subjectively exercise their own ambition for personal gain or power; they keep the benefit of others in their motivation. Neither do they try to use their own inadequate knowledge to do important things. They gather information from other sources and other people before making important decisions.

Most people think the key word of politics is power. If only power exists, if the leaders are not united with the Way, their leadership will become tyranny, dictatorship or an evil force that cannot achieve anything great. Only when power, good policy and the Way or Teh come together can a good administration be run. When the politics of the world do not exercise interference in people's lives, people are able to freely pursue the highest level of spiritual achievement, which is in the range of the ultimate spiritual truth.

Everything in the world changes, but the spiritual truth is everlasting, because spiritual truth itself is a law. All change must follow the law. Therefore, the spiritual truth is the eternal law or eternal Way.

5. When the Integral Way Prevails as the Common Reason of All Lives

People do not know the origin of or reason why many things exist in the world. Nothing provides good reason by itself. Only the subtle spiritual truth provides a good reason for the survival of lives, because the existence of all things comes from natural spiritual source.

The subtle spiritual truth is the common reason of all lives and all things to exist. Spiritual energy is also the common cause for all harmonious life. The spiritual truth is the common principle. On the small scale, there are lots of different reasons for things to form. Different principles and different conditions build or create different individual existences or events. However, natural spirituality is on top of all the small details, small principles, small conditions and small reasons.

The development of the universe happened in harmony. The destination of each individual's development is to attain balance, harmony and equilibrium and move toward perfection. Internally, if the concordance of the mind and spiritual reality is strong, a person's power can reach far and the benefit to the external environment and to oneself is long lasting. If discordance happens, it means the mind is obstructed and does not see the truth. Concordance between the universe and one's physical life, mind, motivation, duty, likes and dislikes is called spiritual concordance with the spiritual reality. Where there is concordance with spiritual reality, the mind of the universe and the mind of the individual embrace each other. This makes the individual enjoy a long, happy life.

People are different because their stages of evolution are different. Some people's spiritual energy is the dominant part of their lives. Those people have a strong spiritual tendency; you do not need to encourage them to look for spiritual teachings. They will look for spiritual books to read, and engage in spiritual study and cultivation even if people try to stop them. Some people are still dominated by the material of ordinary society and do not attain enough spiritual development. Even if you push those people, they are still not interested in spiritual learning. Even people in the same family or in close relationships are in different stages of personal and spiritual evolution. Some people are interested in spirit, and others are not. Spiritual reality does not push the one who is in a different stage, or say that they have to learn to be spiritual. It is not like the religious misunderstanding or creation which says that all people need to follow the same faith, believe in one name or one God. Natural spirituality does nothing about people's faith.

The subtle origin allows all to be expressed in different ways. People express their spirituality in different ways. Different religions are formed when spiritual essence moves through different leaders, people who have had different experiences and have different cultural backgrounds. Thus different ways of explanation are formed, and different religions are created, but that is all expression. The subtle substance behind it has nothing to do with the decoration of external form. The way it is expressed may be accurate or not; the explanation is still not the reality, although it gives a fictitious name to such a reality. A young boy can be called George or John. George or John is a convenient word for people to use, but the boy is still a natural life. There is nothing really fixed about the name.

True spiritual practice directly reaches spiritual unity, which is something that no language can describe, and no differences are perceived. Reaching spiritual unity is the most important spiritual practice. With spiritual unity, all lives are brought about and the creativity of all lives is exercised in a normal way. With spiritual unity, health is expressed; no contortion or sick-mindedness is involved.

Spiritual energy can be observed internally, yet it can also be externally observed. When spirituality is applied externally, it manifests as harmonious order, good management and effective arrangement. It does not matter whether we are talking about managing one's personal life, family, business, government of a nation or government of the world. All types of government are management, and all types of management are government. All government has certain ways to find agreement, support and the following and fellowship of the people. When the ways are correct, the government or management follows spiritual reality.

6. When the Integral Way Prevails in Society

When a society is formed, discipline must be applied. Discipline is necessary to teach the members of a society what is acceptable and unacceptable to the society. Discipline implies the practice of reward and punishment. Reward and punishment, however, must not come from personal emotion or from someone's whim, selfishness or groundless motivation. Reward and punishment, in order to be effective and just, must be applied impartially according to certain pre-determined standards; in other words, it must follow natural spiritual reality in order to be correctly applied. If they follow spiritual truth, true order can be established among people. True order is the goal of society.

When the social mode or social code cannot provide a bridge to harmonious communication and relationship among people, it becomes an external restraint that deprives human nature of healthy development and limits freedom. An incorrect social code is not the correct extension of spiritual energy or Teh.

There are two different approaches toward society or human relationship. One approach is general custom. Another approach is in a specific situation of an individual. Sometimes there is a conflict between general custom and the specific approach. This conflict exists in many large scale situations, in social life or political affairs, with big companies or small companies and so forth. There are big principles which contradict the small principles and small principles which conflict with big principles. However, the subtle law is a process. The subtle law itself is above any principle, big or small, and above conflict. The subtle spiritual truth is also the unity of the general and the specific. The Subtle Way is the unification and communication between all opposing and harmonizing points.

In many societies or nations, one strong leader is the controlling power of the citizens. In such a place, if reward and punishment do not follow spiritual reality, a strong leader may be able to maintain a kind of temporary order built from terror or force. When he weakens or dies, however, the order collapses. An administration that depends upon a strong leader or group of leaders is not fundamental and does not make any lasting contribution. What is fundamental and makes a lasting contribution and what a strong leader needs to do to be able to make a lasting contribution is to follow spiritual reality.

Another nature or virtue of spiritual reality is to be centered, fitting, correct or proper. Whenever a thing is centered, fitting, proper and correct, it expresses spiritual truth. The Ultimate Spiritual Truth is great, most centered, just right. It is the principle of greatness, centeredness and correctness. Although in the relative sphere of society nothing is everlasting, everything must give its best. Every individual is the most truthful foundation of a good society.

A society is organized and formed by different individuals. In a society which follows spiritual reality, each individual strives to reach his or her personal Teh. Here, Teh means the highest internal qualities and characteristics of which a person is capable. Keeping our physical health and our honor in life is one aspect of the practice of Teh. Spiritually, following Spiritual Truth is living with a healthy complete life, not only physical life. Through the practice of Teh, a person follows universal subtle truth and is capable of complete development of one's internal spiritual qualities.

People must live in an environment. To help improve the living environment internally and externally is Teh. When the Integral Way or Subtle Law is applied to society, people respect the public spirit. Public spirit is the attitude of wishing the well-being of all people. People shall select virtuous and capable individuals to handle public affairs. Leaders of this society are respected and trusted because of their virtue. They make peace with all people.

In such a society, people not only love their relatives and care for their own children, they also care about other people. They work to make all young people useful to society, and help the children to grow in a healthy way. They work toward helping all disabled or helpless people have something to do to support their lives. They like to give older people support to be able to finish their physical life happily. In such a society, all men and women know their own duty.

This is not to say that one person must do all these things for all people, but that one finds the area in which to best apply oneself and works hard in that direction.

In a society where the Integral Way prevails, if people do not need something, they do not keep it to themselves, because somebody else may need it. Their talent does not necessarily serve themselves, but it also serves other people. There are no schemes, conspiracies or hidden plans where evil can start. There are no thieves, so robbery cannot happen. People do not even need to lock their doors; they feel safe and sleep reposefully.

The whole society which follows the Integral Way or the Subtle Law will be full of equality, friendliness, harmony and selflessness. All people have their use and all people find a way to help their lives. All people feel safe and are happy with their lives.

If we expand our thought to move from a small society to the big society of the world, and this big society follows spiritual truth, it is called fulfilling the essence of life which has been obtained from the universe. This description points the direction that we hold in our hearts and work toward. It can actually happen in some places where people work for it.

7. When the Integral Way Prevails in Physical Health

When the Integral Way is applied to physical health, three things can be considered. The first is the internal system. The internal system is the physical and spiritual foundation of the body. It is like the roots of one's tree of life. A person's internal roots are the meridians or energy channels, blood vessels, nervous and circulation systems, and organs.

The second thing is smooth communication between all the different kinds of roots. Internally, the internal systems all work smoothly because they communicate with and support one another. This is how the whole body is supported. This communication is a kind of transportation. Each small part supports the whole, and the whole supports all the small parts. This is called wholeness; it happens when all the parts or roots communicate well with each other.

The third thing is called balance. External conditions such as too much heat or too much cold, or internal conditions such as sleeping too much, overeating, straining yourself physically or allowing yourself to become weak are all bad for health. They make the system loose, which creates an opportunity for viruses or germs to attack. It is important to keep the system tight, so that it has a strong immune system or internal protection that can fight those viruses. This brings about the concept or principle of balance. Balance is using things in the right quantities, or keeping internal or external conditions from being too extreme. Balance in internal or external conditions is spiritual law applied to physical health.

8. When the Integral Way Prevails in Self-Development
In order to most deeply understand the position of life in the universe, a person needs spiritual development. With spiritual development, you can exercise the potential of your life, which is to reach the best.

Spiritual learning or cultivation starts from your own spiritual awareness. Step by step, from being far reaching, one finally meets the center of the self or the essence. Develop yourself from your own spiritual center to cover the entirety of the world.

The subtle origin has the power to renew itself continually and constantly. Human spirits also need to learn how to renew their own spirit daily.

9. When the Integral Way Prevails in the Expression of Emotions
Living in the world, each individual faces all kinds of contradictory situations or conflicts. When conflicts or difficult situations arise, the first thing needing to be done is to control one's emotions, such as joy, anger, sorrow and excitement. Before they burst out, or are seen, you must place yourself in neutral. Then when you express them, you will not lose your balance. That is an important principle.

In behavior, you always need to choose the moderate way, the balanced way. Do not do things to extreme. If you learn a good thing, always keep doing it. Once you effectively learn to improve a bad habit such as expressing emotions improperly or thinking wrong thoughts, immediately stop doing that. Although there is difficulty in overcoming habits, the challenge of doing so will make you strong.

The way of life of a true achiever of spiritual truth is simple. Such a person stays in the central point. Those who do not understand spiritual truth, however, do things too much or not enough. In other words, they do things to extremes. So in whatever direction a person is moving, do not lose balance.

From the external change of bad habits and from not going to extremes, a person can reach the innermost spiritual reality and find internal and external unity.

10. When the Integral Way Prevails in the Confidence of Life

The Subtle Origin is the life force of the universe. The life force has a cycle. One sure thing is that all cycles always turn. This offers us a stable understanding about what life holds for us. For example, in deep winter when the cold is severe, the warm spring is on its way.

Let us relate the concept of cyclical motion to human life. For example, when a person is frustrated because of a setback to their plans, there is always a new, sometimes even better opportunity which will come along. For example, when you experience a difficulty, blockage or extremity in your life, you shall see that a good opportunity shall return to you later in a different way.

Spiritual reality is external experience, but it is also internal experience. This means that cycles are not only external, but they are also internal. Cycles sometimes happen at the same time, but sometimes at different times. Sometimes cycles bring benefit and at other times they bring disbenefit. When you see a person engaging in a bad thing, such as a negative confrontation or expression of their destructive nature, then a vicious cycle follows. That means that if anything is done wrongly or incorrectly, the next thing that comes will also be wrong. Then, the situation finally finds its destruction because of the behavior which was applied to look for wrong benefit.

In individual life, the motivation of the mind is the king of all spirits. Through your mind, you decide your reward in life and also decide the punishment of your life. When you find harmony within and without, your life will be rewarded with joy. If you create disharmony, internal or external, in the short run and also throughout the duration of your life, you will be punished. Thus, reward and punishment can be seen to issue from internal sources, although they manifest externally. Therefore, God is both internal and external.

11. When the Integral Way Prevails in Relationship

When you are young, the most important relationship in life is the relationship between yourself and your parents. When you become an adult, it is the relationship with your life partner, your spouse. When you work in society, it is your relationship to the boss or government. Both sides of all relationships look for harmony, unity and cooperation to bring about the positive aspects of life, such as a good condition of life, happiness and prosperity. These could be said to be life's reward. Only mutual understanding, mutual support and mutual service can bring about the reality of a good, lasting relationship.

In achieving this kind of rewarding life and constructive relationships, each individual must look for his or her own kindness, righteousness, politeness, wisdom and trustworthiness. A person who has these five personal characteristics can bring harmony into any situation in which he or she is a creative, helpful member. Such a person will be helpful rather than cause damage, owe something to people or cause disadvantage.

12. When the Integral Way Prevails in Management on a Big or Small Scale

When the Integral Way is applied to a relationship, society, management, administration or government, the return or destination is harmony. If you do not look for harmony, you are only looking for temporary personal achievement; that will cause condemnation and punishment. Therefore, no leader should act without first looking for the agreement of all parts, thus bringing harmony to one's actions. It is important to look not only for the agreement of one's own side and one's supporters, but for harmony in the opposite side and the support of the opposite leaders as well. Then one can find the right weight on the scale for good decision-making.

Looking for agreement from others means a person does not always do what he or she wants or thinks necessary. Sometimes it means adjusting the timing of doing what is necessary to be able to fit the situation. Harmony is the element of cooperation that builds a more enjoyable world. Harmony with one's external environment brings internal peace. Those who can manage to have or maintain a state of internal peace can experience everlasting enjoyment.

Life itself is not limited to the self. The self can be enlarged and developed to cover the entire universe. Spiritual reality is the self nature of an individual; spiritual reality is also the self nature of the universe.

When spiritual truth is applied to measure personal behavior or the decisions of a government, it measures by means of a subtle standard or subtle criterion. When one's behavior or the administration of a government meet that criterion, it is an expression of spiritual truth. Otherwise, it has lost the subtle balance. There is a subtle criteria. The behavior or decision must find coherence with the subtle criteria. That is the Ultimate Spiritual Truth.

13. When the Integral Way Prevails in Practical Life Achievement

When the Integral Way is applied to practical matters or in pursuit of a specific goal, timing is important. General circumstances and specific circumstances are connected, but also have differences. The general circumstance is the subtle and apparent condition of the big environment. The specific circumstance is the subtle and apparent condition of a specific person or matter. However, the general circumstance is the leader, not the mother, of the specific situation. Harmony must be found between the two.

When there is a conflict between moral law and personal emotion, or a conflict between a general circumstance and a specific circumstance, there is a connection between the differences of the two sides in conflict. However, one must respect the moral law or common cause and allow one's feeling and emotion to yield. This means using the big reason to manage the small reason. We must follow the higher law in doing things because this is following the subtle truth. For example, in a marriage relationship, the higher law is to do what is correct. In some marriages this means staying together for the benefit of the children being raised or to fulfill some common goal. In other marriages it means breaking up for the benefit of the children. Yet no person should be too rigid and insist upon their own emotion or feeling. It is only through objectivity that a person will have accomplishment. All reasons and all principles must accept the restraint of time and condition. In other words, when applying a principle to a situation, you must learn to apply it according to the restraints of time and conditions. If the timing for the change is not good, and you do it anyway, it is against the subtle spiritual reality.

14. When the Integral Way Prevails in Understanding the Integral Truth Itself

I would like to offer you a new illustration about the Integral Truth. "The Integral Way is the subtle center, like the hub is the center of a wheel." A hub is the center of a wheel or the central part around which all things move. Similarly, the Integral Truth is the subtle hub of the world and of everything. Everything moves around the hub, moving and circling; the whole wheel itself also has one certain direction forward.

The Integral Truth can also be illustrated by a big city which has a city center or downtown; all roads aim toward the center. The roads that do not aim toward the center connect the roads that do. Thus, we learn that all things intersect one another by themselves, or move by themselves.

In general, I have used the expressions "following the Subtle Law" or "going against the Subtle Law" many times. These expressions can be understood by using the analogy of freeway or highway traffic. "Following the Subtle Law" means you follow the direction of external life, and keep moving - you keep driving your car in the correct direction toward your destination. "Going against the Subtle Law" means you are traveling the wrong way down a one-way street or in the opposite lane of traffic. You enter somewhere against the direction of the one-way alley, street or highway; that will cause collision. That is called moving against the Subtle Law. It is moving against the flow of things as they are.

Thus, it would seem that when you follow the Subtle Law, the Subtle Energy is something external. Then, what is the internal operation that we so often talk about? What is internal behavior? A driver driving a car can also be used as an analogy for internal behavior or operation. Although he drives in the right direction and follows the traffic rules, the important thing for his safety is to concentrate on his driving, and at the same time, pay attention to changes in the road conditions. Although a person is mostly safe in the right lane of traffic, at the same time, you still need to pay attention to what you are doing. This is the internal operation that is so important.

I would like you to understand that the teaching of the Integral Way is different from the teaching of religion. Religions teach a person to believe in a powerful God who is an external Master that can take care of your behavior and your life. In other words, they think that God is a bus driver who will take everybody safely to a certain destination. However, when people receive life, each one is in the driver's seat of their own car. Each person is totally responsible for obtaining correct directions, getting on the right road and constantly watching the traffic conditions. This will enable a person to move toward the correct destination. This brings about independence in responsibility of life.

Although all roads connect with the center of the hub, the center of town is not the road. It is the destination. It is not responsible for taking care of you. You are the one who is responsible for following the road skillfully. I hope this illustration helps clarify the application of your faith or understanding of subtle truth in life.

If you are sitting in somebody else's car, you can relax and enjoy the scenery. Yet, even if you hitchhike or ride in other people's cars, you still need to know what direction you are going in, so as not to allow the car or train to take you in a different direction from where you wish to go.

15. Applying the Integral Way in Your Life Situation and in Mental Control

Concentration is a spiritual condition which is important whether you are driving a car or managing your life. Concentration does not mean to concentrate on an external object; it is concentration upon life itself. It is a power of knowing, an intuitive mystical power which is not obtained by language. It is obtained by keeping your awareness upon the subtle actions that occur inside your thoughts, inside your body, inside the immediate ten inches or so that surround you, and inside your environment. With this mystical intuitive power, you know everything, including the sufficiency of your spiritual nature. This is the way to master your life. When you do so, you can allow all things around you to be what they are. In this way, everything can smoothly reach the Subtle Origin. You join the transformation, but at the same time you maintain the centeredness which is untouched by transformation.

So the true master is in your innermost being; however, whatever you accomplish in your life looks like you have nothing to do with it and receives recognition from the mind before it attains spiritual awareness. Having intuitive power is attained by relaxing one's nervous system and quieting the active intellect. This masterly energy will spontaneously respond to a situation and give the advice you need. An example of this happened in a family. One night the young daughter dreamt that the big tree in their yard was going to fall. She saw the picture of the smashed house. So the young daughter, on the second day, found many ways to convince the whole family to go away. The actual disaster happened that night and the house was totally destroyed. What other name can you give this masterly energy in the most critical time of life? By listening to the advice given intuitively by the subtle spirits, you accomplish life and accomplishing the surroundings of life without interference.

16. Applying the Integral Way in Emotional or Nervous Control

Now let us talk about how to apply the Integral Way to your emotional nervousness. We have learned earlier that the Subtle Origin generates itself. Life and death, prosperity and poverty (or difficulty) are all phenomena of nature. Although nothing can be considered to be predecided, times of difficulty are natural elements of everybody's life. Because they are natural, you do not need to be so nervous about them.

I would like to tell you a story. A businessman had a beloved wife and a son. He always worked hard to support his wife and child, believing that they could not live without the effort he made to support them. However, it happened that a northern tribe invaded the southern part of the country. When everything was in chaos, the northern tribe took the man captive and carried him away. The man was worried; he thought his wife and son would soon be finished without his being there with them. How could they live? So he kept a troubled mind. The northern tribe used him as a bookkeeper, saw his earnest characteristics and saw that he was under emotional pressure from worrying about his family. There was no way that communication could be established with his family any more. So they found a woman for the man to marry. They married, and had a child; then the man had the same worry about his new wife and child that he had about his wife and child in the south.

Fifteen or sixteen years later, both sons were attending school and passed the governmental examination. They both became government officials and met each other. Before long, they found out they had the same father. It was the meeting of the two sons that reminded the father after so long that he had two wives and two sons. Originally, he kept worrying because he did not believe that anything could live without his care, but finally he came to see that everyone had a happy ending.

This shows that sometimes people are so nervous, they think the world cannot keep going on without them. However, times of difficulty are natural to life, so none of them need to be so emotionally worried.

Many people suffer from nervousness. They do not see that if they do nothing wrong, and if everything follows the subtle law, things will grow naturally. There is a kind of natural assurance that everything will grow, and everything will enjoy its development in its own way.

17. The Application of the Integral Way in the Pursuit of a Name

For many artistic or professional people, it is important to have a name. For some of them the name becomes the goal of their lives, so they work hard only wishing to earn a name. Some people are lucky enough to earn a name, but most people struggle with their artistic effort and do not achieve what they expected. Is having a name important? Having a name means having a good reputation.

We must know that the words "Subtle Origin" are the words we apply to something that cannot be specifically defined. It would be better if the Subtle Origin had no name at all, because it has no definition. The Subtle Truth can be anything; the Subtle Truth can be nothing. It exists as universal prime energy. Sometimes people call the Subtle Truth God, but that really narrows the conception of spiritual truth, because spiritual truth is everywhere. Most people conceive of God as an individual, a big father in the sky; he cannot be everywhere. However, the Subtle Origin is connected with each life. It is so important, but it has no name. If it has no name, then why do we call it by a name such as the spiritual truth or the Integral Way? We use a name so we can think about it. Yet the spiritual truth is beyond conception.

Differences are not more important than the common reality that exists behind all differences. The Subtle Truth is such a reality. In the West, maybe the Subtle Truth is called God or something else. However, the names are not reality; they are not the real thing. A thing or object can have different names. An idea or a concept can also have different names. For example, in English, you say "yes." In Chinese, yes is "shr." In Spanish it is "si." In German, it is called "ya." Which one is correct? All of them, and none of them, so names are not definite. People also have different names for the Subtle Truth: God, Allah, Great Spirit, Love, Dios, Jehovah, etc.

Those who are crazy about having a name should remain natural. This means that if you do what is natural for you to do, the name will come by itself. You will not have to struggle to earn the name, it will just happen. It is all right to have a name, but it is also all right not to have one. If you cannot have a name, do not fight and struggle to have one, such as by bad creation or behavior, but improve your real art, the real essence of life.

A name is attached to the essence of what you are. Because no external thing - such as a name - is essential, then why are you worrying about external things? Being nobody is essential. Being somebody is secondary.

18. When the Integral Way Is Applied in Achieving Your Social Goal

If you are helpful, if your service really reaches the true goal of helping, you do not need to fight. All strength will come to you to accomplish the task, and you will become more powerful. If you are not engaged in a working endeavor, the best thing is to manage yourself. Self-aggrandizement is a sickness, a spiritual undevelopment which blocks true leadership or management.

If you are naturally in a position of strength or leadership and you cannot excuse yourself from accomplishing certain tasks, you must do your best to follow natural law and guide the world to peace. Only a peaceful world can bring prosperity or a good life to all people.

Intention is important for people in the position of leadership. In truthful natural psychology, a special term "I" (ee) is given to describe the intention or subtle intention within oneself. To accomplish any type of leadership, or for that matter any kind of general activity, you first need a good intention before you start to move or act.

In the cultivation of spiritual energy, if we are disturbed by having many different or conflicting intentions, our cultivation can become difficult. Intentions are an automatic response or reaction to one's environment. For example, if you go out the door, and you see that the doorway is dirty, you might automatically sweep it. If you see that your flowerbed has some grass in it, you might automatically reach over to do some weeding.   If you continue doing a myriad of activities all day long, then when you close your eyes to meditate or sit quietly, you are still busy from one intention transferred to a second intention.   The intention brings about memory, association from past experiences and so forth.

Intention itself is an energy.   Intention is giving a direction to one's energy.   Once the direction is set, your whole body reacts internally.   Therefore, establish your spiritual unity and watch your intentions so you will not get pulled out by unimportant or wrong ones.

Most intentions in life are a response to external environmental or internal pressure.   Usually the intention is worldly.   Once the entirety of your life being is at peace with your particular intention, the intention receives the whole support of your life energy.   This complete energy converges so that the task can be accomplished.

19.   When the Integral Way Prevails as the Subtle Substance of Life

The subtle essence of life is the same energy as the immortal substance which enables you to fly over the rainbow and fly with light. You can reach anywhere with light. It is one possibility of what a person can do with one's life energy.

All life is decided by the subtle substance that lives within itself. If the subtle substance leaves the life, the body becomes a shell and there is no more life. So the reality of life is how strong the subtle substance is.   If a person's strong physical worldly intentions are controlled, naturally the strong subtle substance can be turned around to reach the stage of immortality. That is important. The application of the Integral Way in spiritual cultivation has the purpose of immortality or universal broad spiritual experience that proves the reality or possibility of immortality.

20.   When the Integral Way Prevails in Social Equality and Personal Achievement

When the Integral Way is applied to social classes, it does not emphasize equality.   Also, it does not support the establishment of differences among classes or people. The key word is "natural." This means that equality is the external demand of society after society's naturalness has been lost. In reality, there are differences between each of the people in society, but being natural still means equality, at least spiritually. For example, in the sky, there are big stars and small stars. The big stars shine more brightly than the small stars, but all have their positions.

Similarly, each individual has his or her own spiritual potential, but the spiritual potential of each individual is not equal. This means that people are capable of doing different tasks or jobs in life.

21. When the Integral Way Prevails as the Subtle Path of Spiritual Development

In spiritual potential, we sometimes talk about equal opportunity. External demands can be established for people to do certain things like pursue certain careers, but they are not natural. Some people have to work hard all their lives to achieve themselves and earn their own life reward. Others are born into a family with a life environment which already provides all the rewards, and so the people do not need to work. You can observe this reality in your neighborhood, society or anywhere. People are born into different situations, so the ideal of external equality cannot really be established.

Superficially, people are on equal ground, although it is not truthful because their development is different. Even if everybody is standing at the same altitude, some people are still taller or shorter. Some are more intelligent or more physical than others. All have different benefits and different contributions to offer society.

Fighting for equality in modern society is meaningful because conventional society established classes. In a natural society, social classes were not established, so nobody could attract attention or support by using equality as a slogan for war, revolution or social movement. In a natural society, equality is meaningless. Because we live in the United States, a country which respects the concept of equality, personal development is important.   Personal development decides where and what one is.

I do not recommend that you fight or refuse to be where you are now; I only recommend that you develop yourself.   Wherever you are, you do not need to resent whatever life opportunities do or do not come to you. Instead, value the opportunity at hand to further develop yourself.   That is an important message in learning the Integral Way.

Although people are equal, the reality of life is that people have differences in intelligence, physical constitution, spiritual tendencies, and the like. Because of those differences in human structures, it is not possible to take the idea of equality to an extreme. Systems of government such as communism which try to do this must fail because they are unnatural.   Communism causes the loss of people's incentive to improve or better themselves. In truth, even in communist society, there is no equality; the treatment is secretly different because some people hold more power than others. Social equality in a communist system was an ideal; it can never be fully achieved.   When ungrounded idealism is applied to human life, unnaturalness occurs. Anything unnatural is evil and sometimes causes trouble.

22.   The Integral Way Cannot Be Applied as External Beliefs

When a person who lives in the world as a leader or as an individual can control his or her life situation, it is called, "Using nothing to govern something." This principle means being objective or empty minded to eliminate preconception about how to handle all situations. If you eliminate preconception, everything you need will come to you. In that way, you will be an excellent manager of your life. It means, specifically, treat each thing according to its own nature without asserting any personal dogma or attitude.

It is acceptable for people to have religious faith if they do not try to impose their immature beliefs onto other people, but real growth can only be attained when they are able to see the conflict between real life situations and unreasonable religious ideas or beliefs. If they hold to their beliefs, they become slaves to them. They miss the reality of life. The inability of people to connect their beliefs to the reality of life can be resolved through learning the Subtle Truth. The Subtle Integral Way is the point at which life and belief meet. It is the balanced approach to both belief and life activity.

Every day, people engage in certain life activity or no activity. What is the connection between one's everyday life activities and spiritual truth? The answer is simple. Spiritual truth is what you can find in all life activities: all proper and suitable behavior. Natural Spiritual Truth is within all suitable behavior and rightful activity in your life.

23. When the Integral Way Is Applied to the Frame of Cause and Effect, It Is Achievement

In general life and behavior, the recognition of cause and effect can be established. When the kind of cause is established, then it can be known what kind of effect will be created by the cause. As you sow, you shall reap.

For example, if a person is at point A and wishes to go to point B, he will start upon the route to his destination. However, he cannot actually see point B. To learn the Integral Way is to learn the way to reach point B from point A. It means setting out in the correct direction, and altering or changing one's course as necessary to continue on the way. When the course is changed, the effect or direction also will be changed, thus the effect will be changed. Nevertheless, if one has a good result or intention as one's goal, this is not a negative statement, because one can bring about a better effect by making good changes in the course. If a person has a certain goal, changing the course can bring about either fulfilling or unfulfilled achievement.

But if the same cause is applied to different people, it will bring about different effects. In other words, if two people set out for the same destination, the paths they travel and the places they actually reach will be different. The difference comes from the differences in the people and also the paths each one travels on. It is the middle stage or process that is important. By this I mean, the way one travels from point A to point B is the Integral Way or the true path. It is different for each person.

In general, people accept the law of cause and effect. The cause is what reaches the effect. Nevertheless, most people ignore or neglect the process or the way between the cause and the effect, the path or route, in traveling from A to B. For example, a young man loves a young woman; that is the cause of a friendship or relationship. However, the cause does not necessarily bring about a positive effect, and even though it might bring the effect of marriage, it may be a good marriage or a bad marriage. Therefore, the cause did not decide the effect. The decisive factor is the process.

The process is not the cause, the process is the way from the cause to effect, the route from point A to point B. A cause can be set, and a goal can also be set as the effect of the motivated cause. Yet, in fulfilling the effect, the process is changeable and must be managed.

For example, let us say that somebody gives you an orchid plant, a gorgeous orchid plant with flowers. Orchids are usually grown on a piece of board. The cause is owning the plant with desire for it to produce flowers, so you might expect the plant to give you flowers again sometime later. Its process of living may bring a good result or it may not. For example, you might overwater it or you might not water it enough. Either situation will damage the plant.

So you can also consider the process as the cause in depth. First you know that point A is the cause, then there is a process, then point B is the effect. Then you know the effect is safely reached by the process. Now you see that the process is the most important factor in bringing about a desirable effect.

Most people think that the cause is receiving or buying the orchid. They do not see that the correct process - which is taking care of the flowering plant - is what brings about good fruit or a good flower.

Let us use another example. If you buy stock, the stock does not decide if you will become rich. The process of when you buy and sell the stock determines whether you make or lose money. If you bought and sold some stock at the right time and you made money, was it your destiny? It was not destiny, it was the application of your knowledge and your energy in the right way and at the right time. It was the process.

Many people think that the goal of life is to become rich or noble. This concept does not totally agree with the Integral Way. It agrees with the Integral Way only when your profit or benefit also benefits other people. In other words, it also depends upon the process.

In one of the western states, there is a ditch that was used by a seeker of gold. During the last century, a Chinese man came along and hired many other Chinese people to dig that ditch. He wished to become rich by filtering the sandy water to find gold. At that time, the Manchurian government in mainland China required all men to grow their hair long and wear it in a braid behind their head. It had become a social fashion, like women binding their feet. This man hired people who came from China, and he would shave their hair or cut their braid off, so they had to work for him for a certain length of time before they could return to China without embarrassment. That person surely got lots of gold, but he treated people badly. He only wished to become rich by himself.

What happened? He did not wish to be rich in a foreign country, he wanted to bring his riches home so he could enjoy himself more. He took the gold back to China. When he got there, people caught him and beat him to death because he had treated them so evilly. The moral of this story is that if you wish to become rich, if you want to stay safe and be able to enjoy yourself, treat other people fairly.

I believe that the man in this story was a capable and intelligent person. He knew how to make people work, but who was benefitted? He did not benefit himself, because the way he achieved his goal was against the Integral Way. So those who follow the Integral Way can look for profit, but they also like to see other people enjoy a certain amount of profit too.

A student of the Subtle Truth does not watch the cause and effect, he or she watches the process. A good, right process can bring about a good result.

Some political systems have as their goal a society of total equality. They want to see equal opportunity in work and pay. They do not want some people to work less than others. Still, despite their attempts to require equality, people work differently because some people are more intelligent, capable, or spirited than others. The goal of rewarding people fairly for their work in different positions with different pay is correct. What I would like to point out here is that success in achieving such a good society can be had if the political leaders look at the process. By constantly making corrections in the route or path - which here means policy and administration - they could achieve the fairness they desire without rigidly imposing unfair standards of equality. In order to reach the true achievement, they must adapt to the reality of the country's situation. Thus, you can see that the adjustable process is what decides the success of the system so that all can enjoy rightfully. The process will change the reality of the original purpose, and make it better if they are attentive. Therefore, watching the ongoing process of a work and taking care of the process of a matter is the most important part. It is even more important than the cause and the effect themselves. In other words, the Subtle Integral Way is more important than the cause or motivation, and effect or goal.

24. When the Integral Way Prevails in Learning the Integral Way Itself

The most important learning of all is to learn the Subtle Truth. The process or Way of learning Subtle Truth is different from external learning. Learning Spiritual Truth depends upon self-awareness. Self-awareness is an expression of spiritual self-nature. Once one's personal self-nature is strong enough, it can reflect itself, but it cannot see itself. Only when it is put in a situation - put in front of a mirror as it were - can it see itself. Spiritual cultivation and spiritual awareness are the Way to reach the Subtle Origin.

Spiritual learning happens step by step. A person starts by learning and then achieves the ability to apply good learning or good knowledge to everyday life. This happens by having the honesty to see what is incorrect or does not work well in your life and replace it with something that works better.   By remaining pure and sincere, by watching your mind and not letting it go in the wrong direction, you can always correct or inspect yourself and rectify improper behavior. This is how to cultivate yourself. It will also help your family members, society and the world.

25. When the Integral Way Prevails to Reach Freedom

The Subtle Origin is the deep root of life. The Subtle Origin is the deep root of the universe. Nobody and nothing can escape the law of nature - the Subtle Law - because it is the law of the universe. The freedom that can be achieved through spiritual cultivation is not done under the restraint of any artificial demand. Only when you become the law and join the being of the subtle law can you have freedom.

The attainment of Spiritual Truth is embodied in developing your spirit to become the subtle law. When you become one with the subtle law, you do not know you exist any more. The subtle law is an immortal; it has freedom above all things. A being who exists above the subtle law is an immortal, a highly achieved spiritual being. Beings who extend outside or beneath the subtle law are mortal. Because they are not within the subtle law, they must accept its governing. If they do not accept its governing, they sometimes suffer. The way to stop being governed by the subtle law is to learn to manage your life, restrain your impulse, and discipline the overflow of your life energy.

On the way to attaining Spiritual Truth, you will come up against places you cannot go through. Your road is stopped by being something or holding something. This is common, but it can be avoided or overcome. To unite with the Integral Way or the Ultimate Subtle Law, you have to empty yourself. If you have any preconception, philosophical conception or particular idea, it will become a barrier, and then you cannot go through. To be with and unite with the Spiritual Truth is to empty your preconceptions and whatever small or big intentions or ambitions you have. This is how you can become the Spiritual Truth.

Following the Integral Way is being wise and being clear. Clarity and high wisdom is the Integral Truth. The

Integral Spiritual Truth is attainable. Once your mind attains clarity, once your mind attains wisdom, you can apply it either to a particular circumstance or to the big scale of absolute truth. The wisdom you reach for is all based on clarity of mind.

We already know that human nature is an extension of universal nature. Humanistic nature raised above animal nature is the spiritual development of human people. Developed human nature is brought about by spiritual development.

If you observe society at any time in history, you will see that people always have trouble. Internally, in looking for external pursuit, people lose their spiritual self-nature. They are affected by social fashion, the time, society, customs or pressures in life, and thus each individual loses their own self-nature. The restoration of original self-nature is one important process in eliminating all contamination and temptation against spiritual nature. If a person restores his own self-nature, he will not be so motivated or tempted by social fashion, unnecessary custom or life circumstances which will cause one to deviate from the Subtle Truth.

Sometimes people's behavior comes from jealousy, ignorance or greed. They all reflect loss of self-nature. Self-nature is experiencing contentment with what you have and what you are; it is not looking at what other people have. If you do not serve the center of life in individual self as human spiritual nature, then what else do you serve in order to satisfy your life?

People's self-nature is contained in the balance of three dimensions: physical, mental and spiritual, none of which should be overly extended. The balance of all three in an individual life is following the Integral Way. The restoration of complete individual self-nature is one important goal of spiritual learning. The Way to restore self-nature is through learning the Subtle Truth.

26. When the Integral Way Prevails in Destiny

Many people think that destiny decides whether an individual will become rich, noble, prosperous or successful in life. Astrology can tell each individual's position in the solar energy at birth. Although it is certainly an important influence, the formula provided by astrology and the energies it represents are not the only influence in a person's life. Because we live on earth, we affect one another's individual nature. This can be seen through spiritual development. People such as twin brothers or twin sisters, or even close neighbors in the same apartment building born in the same sun sign, may have different lives. Many conventional people believe that destiny or fortune determine a person's life, but that belief is not totally accurate. For example, becoming noble or rich is not entirely decided by fortune or astrology; it is also decided by people themselves.

Conclusion

The natural harmonious order in the universe is rationality or reason. This natural rationality expresses itself in the human mind as wisdom. In nature, you see rationality through the harmony, balance, orderliness, symmetry and centeredness of the natural environment. This natural rationality or reason is God itself. What else could you call God? It is the master energy of nature. When this Masterly energy reveals itself in the human mind, it is commonly recognized as rational power. This is the source of true teaching of the Integral Way.

Many times I refer to the wisdom of the ancient, naturally achieved people. In a certain way of looking at it, they had no achievement because their wisdom was natural; nothing was forced or contrived. They accepted rational energy as the only master to which all people are subject.

When I teach the rational integral truth, I often discuss human spirituality and religion, because truth is not actually separated from anything. The subtle law is in everything and every event. However, religions are different from the subtle law. Religions are an approach to help you conduct your impulse and emotion in an unknown direction. Usually, religions guide people in a direction opposite the spiritual truth, to a place where there is no balance, harmony, orderliness or symmetry. It is a place with no spiritual centeredness; instead, it creates religious drama.

In true practice of the Integral Way, we follow the ageless master 太上老君. Who is the 'highest old master'? Where do you go to search for the Integral Way? It is often seen that religions misguide or misdirect people to go where they can never contact the true master. "The true master" has been discussed by Chuang Tzu. If you do not read carefully, you may miss it, because there is much discussion about many things in his book.

The terms I use in my teaching - Heaven, God, the Great One, Integral Truth, Tao, and the like are all descriptions for what I exalt: the true Master of all. That is the Integral Way. Spiritual reality is infinite, not finite, thus spiritual law can be applied to all situations. Religions are not spiritual truth; religions are finite. Thus, they guide people to adopt duality in religious practice and in daily life.

Another key word used in my teaching is "nature." Nature is important, because the human mind tends to rationalize things in its life experience. This causes inaccurate descriptions of reality, because rationalization is not natural. Rationalization is defending from admitting one's mistake or shortcoming. This tendency toward self-defense damages natural clear vision and correct rational thinking. Lao Tzu described in his teaching that by not allowing the mind to be too active, you will allow natural rationality to be as it is, undisturbed. In other words, if you actively disturb, reorganize or rearrange your mind, you do not find true spirituality. When you attempt to rationalize reality, you move away from spiritual balance; thus, you lose yourself.

I have said, as other ancient teachers have said before me, Spiritual Reality is nothing, or following the Subtle Law is doing nothing. Please learn to see the importance of nothing and doing nothing. I have been doing a lot and saying a lot, but I also have been doing nothing and saying nothing. Where else can you catch nothing? When you attempt to catch it, the masterly energy disappears.

This seems contradictory. It sounds like I am implying that you can catch nothing, then implying that you cannot catch it. This is because people do not see that nothingness is not void, but it just looks void. It is indescribable; it is neither a wave nor a particle. It is the foundation of all existence, but it cannot be separated from anything. It is the Integral Truth. When you poise yourself in composure, the Integral Truth - or nothing - is there with you.

This type of truthful teaching is hard for most people to understand. Thus, the ancient achieved teachers introduced nothingness by teaching the ultimate law of yin and yang. When their students did not think that they had learned enough, then the teachers started to teach the three spheres: physical, mental and spiritual, which cover all things. True teachers know that all three return to unity of all three. Although the three are within all things, the three also return to be one. Finally, all returns to be spirit.

The human mind has at least three elements: 1) intellect or knowledge, 2) affection, and 3) will or desire. These three are one; they function differently but return to be one.

The "true master" is not like world rulers who impose themselves over others. The true master functions only when you allow it to exercise its function. Yet, all are subject to it because it is the source of all. When people do not enjoy a state of well-being, the master is weak or incorrectly positioned. The master itself does not impose or establish itself. It exists and manifests when the application of all levels of mind finds normalcy and prosperity in all situations. It is in normalcy and prosperity that the true master is in control. When the application of mind misses centeredness and balance, a partial energy is too strong, and this energy is not aligned with one's own true nature.

Spiritual teaching, governmental service and the direction of social politics are not evil when aligned with the true master, which I also call the subtle law or Integral Way. Integral Way is achieved through spiritual development.

Each individual has a three-level mind. The true master is the highest of the three levels. Some people choose to live in solitude in order to serve only the true master. Solitude is not necessary, but usually one's environment must at least be manageable. However, most of us do not have these conditions, so we must live in the rough world. We need to learn to flow with the world by attuning our mind to the center or point where our internal and external energy meet harmoniously.

The easy way to live is to be natural, truthful and considerate, in all occasions. If you live that way, you attune yourself to spiritual reality every day and in every moment. If you do it all the time, it becomes so natural that there is no need of effort. Thus, you are practicing Wu Wei.

Nevertheless, even righteous people who do so sometimes suffer from trouble caused by others. Because people understand things differently, each society needs laws and a judicial system. In a direct conflict or difficulty, speaking for oneself is not effective, and needs a third party such as a lawyer or judge. Yet the subtle law is still higher than any human law or court. The subtle law relates deeply with a person's own spiritual development. People may not know it, but they live with the subtle law. Only when people's natural virtue becomes unnatural is the subtle law misunderstood or apparently damaged. To resolve conflict, I do not suggest that peace be made by sacrificing righteousness but to look for the point of balance. Even when an individual is right, it is necessary to be in a position of strength before yielding one's position, exercising kindness, or forgiving the wrongdoer.

Many kinds of people make up the world. Some people are unreasonable. Some things make no sense. Still, sometimes it is necessary to live with unreasonable people and senseless things. If you can choose to avoid them, it is wise to do so. If you cannot avoid them, it is wise to find a way to moderate your contact with them. Discipline and moderation in a conflict is practicing kindness and tolerance. It is not great to take in all energy. What greater truth can you live with to refine yourself?

Religions teach holiness because religious leaders think the world is unholy. The concept of holiness relies upon the support of the unholy, which produces a dualistic practice.

Following spiritual teachings is not a matter of being holy or unholy. Everything has a natural reason for living, but improvement and development is needed by all. The Subtle Law accepts all and accepts nothing. Therefore, Spiritual Truth is not damaged when it lives with things. Spiritual Truth is not arrogant, but finds contentment and completeness in itself.

Chapter 7

Learning from Two Great Masters

I

In this book, I have given two versions of Master Kou Hong's life and in the second volume of this book, I have given two versions of Master Chen Tuan's life. I would like to call to your attention something about the way biographies of people are told. In the first version, Master Kou Hong's life was colored with the literary brush. I adopted and adjusted it from the popular story in which at least some stories of other individual lives were combined and confused as one person. The life experience of two other important people were mixed with that of Kou Hong. For example, the magic performance is from the biography of Kou Hong's granduncle, Master Kou Shuan, and the practice of alchemy to turn the cheap metal into gold is from Prince Liu An, plus the real Kou Hong.

However, in both versions, I did not mention the important contribution Master Kou Hong made to Chinese medicine. The description of Master Kou Hong's internal practice is also shallowly touched. Regarding the use of certain points or spots on the body in spiritual cultivation, only the point between the two eyebrows was mentioned. In reality, in internal spiritual practice, many important points are used or focused upon for different effects and purposes. The other popular ones have locations such as: 1) the point between the two eyes (which is different from the point between the two eyebrows); 2) the three tan tien (tan tien means the field of producing internal medicine.) They are the centers of the three main sections of the body: the head, chest and abdomen; 3) the vital gate (on the back of the navel); 4) the middle soul terrace (the back of the middle tan tien); 5) the jade pillow (the rear center of the head); and 6) the point of 1,000 meeting (there are two points of meeting; the one for yang energy is on the top of the head and the one for yin energy is between the two legs. They are linked by the middle tunnel of the trunk of the body and the center of the spinal cord). This is, of course, not a complete list of all the points used in spiritual cultivation, but these are some of the main ones. All such points are important in natural spiritual cultivation on different stages for different purposes. In the first story, only the point between the eyebrows was introduced, but it is not suitable for people who have high blood pressure or hypertension. The points used or chosen became esoteric teaching in all generations.

The point between the two eyebrows is an effective point to use for nurturing spiritual energy, but people who have high blood pressure or hypertension should not choose this point. High blood pressure or hypertension is a disease that needs to be cured separately. Many people who did sitting meditation died because of high blood pressure. Dying will cause confusion about the healthy result of meditation. Kundalini yoga has a similar shortcoming - people die. Spiritual cultivation should not be done at noon, in hot weather or in a hot region. Energy connects with life and death. The flow of bodily energy needs to be well conducted. This means it is best to attain correct knowledge and learn from the experience of achieved ones.

Most important is the connection between all the points, because the secret to successful cultivation is to use one point to dam your energy flow. This is done by visualization. In other words, it means to accumulate and strengthen your energy through the intercourse of internal energy.

The strengthening of one's energy is achieved by internal visualization by turning your visual power to a certain internal point. Every day we send out so much energy through the eyes, the windows. It is important knowledge that the subtle energy is scattered by overusing the eyes, thus, conversely, one can make that energy stronger by internally focusing on a certain spot. Generally, when this is done, a response from the nervous system, such as a muscular twitching, may occur but the purpose of doing the focusing is not to twitch. The purpose of the internal visualization is to build up your strong internal energy.

When you wish to do such visualization, take a sitting or lying position. I do not recommend doing it while you are engaged in worldly activities, because they would be a distraction. Do not fall asleep or allow your mind to be random and wandering; otherwise the effect of the practice will be totally nullified. If you do this practice before you sleep at night, wait several minutes after finishing your practice before going to sleep.

Sitting and lying spiritual cultivation was practiced by Masters Kou Hong and Chen Tuan respectively. The interesting thing about spiritual cultivation is that it does not really even need any special position, although special positions can be helpful to some. Just being quiet is usually a realistic enough approach.

Only one stage of Kou Hong's cultivation was discussed in the version of his life. The other parts are important in the progress of a person's cultivation, but only the most important aspect was given in this biography.

In the literary version of Master Kou Hong's life, some of the practices from the later immortal school called "The School of Golden Immortal Medicine" which was founded by Master Lu, Tung Ping and his teachers and students were included or mixed together with his life. Only truly achieved ones who do the practices from that school understand it. The details of these practices were not given in this version in order not to mislead people who would otherwise misunderstand the instruction.

So you can see that in biographies, things are sometimes changed or made to be more colorful or dramatic than they are in real life. I myself have greater respect for the real, unadorned story of Kou Hong - the life of a simple man and the way he cultivated himself - rather than the story that has been decorated with cosmetics. The literary version is more interesting for some people to read, but does not accurately reflect his life. As I see it, it is more important to respect the real Kou Hong than Kou Hong with cosmetics.

Kou Hong proved to be a true realizer of the Integral Way who respected the original value of life more than anything else. The other fulfillments of his practice - the alchemy of base metals, the contribution to Chinese medicine, and magic performance - are just a supplement or an aside to what is more important: the insistence on the original value of life. Many practices mentioned in his book,

Pau Po Tzu, are not the principal practice. This also means that to attain the Integral Way, a learner can skip having to learn how to refine mental into gold, make a contribution to the medical field or learn magic practice. One can save lots of time and trouble and just go directly to the true life practice, unless doing those things are also your destiny. Everybody has a working destiny as well as a spiritual destiny.

Kou Hong is an example of what we might call a true spiritual hermit or a natural recluse. The idea of a hermit to an achieved one is a little different from what westerners might believe a hermit is. It does not mean a person who totally avoids the world. A spiritual recluse is a person who avoids big social involvement and does engage in unnecessary disturbance of meaningless or wasteful struggles among the crowds. Such struggles usually reflect competition for a better social position. A spiritual hermit absolutely keeps away from this. In other words, a natural, spiritual hermit lives the quiet life of an ordinary person in society and avoids political or social gatherings as well as intense struggle to climb the ladder of success. A true spiritual hermit does not hide from the world, but lives in society and avoids being distinguished by worldly honor.

The key to a true life of the Integral Way is to respect the original value of life. True realizers of the Integral Way do not engage in decorating life or in exalting customs. Nor do they put a different value upon it, such as in trying to gain popularity in society or having the largest personal line of credit, etc. The naturalness and wholeness of life itself is what is of value to a real achieved one. This is a key point. It determines whether a person truthfully understands the value of life or engages in meaningless pursuit.

Not all spiritually achieved people become teachers or leaders. The famous Taoist poet, Cold Mountain, was widely accepted and appreciated by Japanese and western Zahn (Zen) practitioners because he lived the lifestyle of a spiritual hermit, although the supreme Master Chuang Tzu was the real initiating master of Zahn (Zen). He made a great achievement and contribution to the transcendental spirit of both Taoism and Zahn Buddhism. These two individuals,

Cold Mountain and Master Chuang Tzu, were not limited by the background of their societies nor by the historical epoch in which they lived. Their writings are an important spiritual contribution for many generations of students of spirituality. Their writings have helped them learn to live differently than society, in a more correct way.

It is hard for a true achieved one of modern times to live like the poet Cold Mountain. He lived a hermetic and impoverished life in the mountains. I do not think his lifestyle is a healthy or correct way to live in modern times. Master Chuang Tzu had a group of students who were supportive and continued his teaching. The writings and life of Chuang Tzu portrayed how the achieved one values life. However, because of the tremendous difference between ancient and modern life, it is not appropriate for modern students and teachers to live in this fashion either. Times have changed. A more balanced lifestyle is needed for modern realizers of the Integral Way.

In real life, I believe Master Kou Hong and Master Chen Tuan make a fresher example for modern people who are looking for balanced fulfillment in life. They each had a true, good natural life with high spiritual achievement and fulfillment of worldly obligation. It is my sincere recommendation as a fellow student and learner of the Integral Way that you understand the balanced, regretless life of these masters.

When I was younger, I found Master Kou Hong and Master Chen Tuan among all the achieved ones as a source of inspiration. Now that I am older, and have paid the price to learn and achieve myself, I can see that many of my personal life experiences and the direction of my life have actually been like episodes of their lives. I have not in any way tried to model my life after them; it is the innate nature in all of us that brings the similarity. Thus, in serving the world, I offer the stories of the lives of these two masters to express truthful traditional values and respect for life. I wish that all of you might know what a spiritual life really is.

About Hua-Ching Ni

Hua-Ching Ni is fully acknowledged and empowered by his own spiritual attainment rather than by external authority. He is a teacher of natural spiritual truth and a natural person. He is heir to the wisdom transmitted through an unbroken succession of numberless generations of true masters dating back to the time before written history. As a young boy, he was educated by his family in the foundation of the natural spiritual truth. Later, he learned spiritual arts from various achieved teachers, some of whom have a long traditional background, and fully achieved all aspects of ancient science and metaphysics.

In addition, 38 generations of the Ni family worked as farmers, natural healers and scholars. Master Ni has continued in America with clinics and the establishment of Yo San University of Traditional Chinese Medicine. Master Ni worked as a traditional Chinese doctor and taught spiritual learning on the side as a service to people. He taught first in Taiwan for 27 years by offering many publications in Chinese and then in the United States and other Western countries since 1976. To date, he has published about thirty books in English, made five videotapes of gentle movement and has written some natural spiritual songs sung by an American singer.

Hua-Ching Ni lived in the mountains at different stages. When possible, he stays part-time in seclusion in the mountains and part-time in the city doing work of a different nature. He believes this is better for his nervous system than staying in only one type of environment.

The books that he has written in Chinese include two books about Chinese medicine, five books about spiritual self-cultivation and four books about the Chinese internal school of martial arts. These were published in Taiwan. He has also written two unpublished books on ancient spiritual subjects related with natural health and spiritual development.

The other unpublished books were written by brush in Chinese calligraphy during the years he attained a certain degree of achievement in his personal spiritual cultivation. He said, "Those books were written when my spiritual energy was rising to my head to answer the deep questions in my mind. In spiritual self-cultivation, only by nurturing your own internal spirit can communication exist between the internal and external gods. This can be proven by your personal spiritual stature. For example, after nurturing your internal spirit, through your thoughts you contact many subjects which you could not reach in ordinary daily life. Such spiritual inspiration comes to help when you need it. Writings done in good concentration are almost like meditation and are one fruit of your cultivation. This type of writing is how internal and external spiritual communication can be realized. For the purpose of self-instruction, writing is one important practice of the Jing Ming School or the School of Pure Light. It was beneficial to me as I grew spiritually. I began to write when I was a teenager and my spiritual self-awareness had begun to grow."

In his books published in Taiwan, Hua-Ching Ni did not give the details of his spiritual background. It was ancient spiritual custom that all writers, such as Lao Tzu and Chuang Tzu, avoided giving their personal description. Lao Tzu and Chuang Tzu were not even their names. However, Master Ni conforms with the modern system of biographies and copyrights to meet the needs of the new society.

Hua-Ching Ni's teaching differs from what is generally called Taoism, conventional religious Taoism or the narrow concept of lineage or religious mixture of folk Taoism. His teaching is non-conventional and differs from the teaching of any other teachers. He teaches spiritual self-sufficiency rather than spiritual dependence.

Master Ni shares his own achievement as the teaching of rejuvenated original spiritual truth, which has its origins in the prehistoric stages of human life. His teaching is the Integral Way or Integral Truth. It is based on the Three Scriptures of ancient spiritual mysticism: Lao Tzu's *Tao Teh Ching, The Teachings of Chuang Tzu* and *The Book of Changes.* He has translated and elucidated these three classics into versions which carry the accuracy of the valuable ancient message. His other books are materials for different stages of learning the truth. He has also absorbed all the truthful high spiritual achievements from various schools to assist the illustration of spiritual truth with his own achieved insight on each different level of teaching.

The ancient spiritual writing contained in the Three Scriptures of ancient spiritual mysticism and all spiritual books of many schools were very difficult to understand, even for Chinese scholars. Thus, the real ancient spiritual teaching from the oriental region is not known to most scholars of later generations, the Chinese people or foreign translators. It would have become lost to the world if Hua-Ching Ni had not rewritten it and put it into simple language. He has practically revived the ancient teaching to make it useful for all people.

BOOKS IN ENGLISH BY MASTER NI

Life and Teaching of Two Immortals, Volume 1: Kou Hong - *New Publication!*
Master Kou Hong was an achieved Taoist Master born into an ordinary family around 283 A.D. in China. He was the first master of Tao to write an important book with details about immortal practice. He was also a healer in Traditional Chinese Medicine and a specialist in the art of refining medicines, including immortal medicine. Master Kou Hong successfully refined his golden immortal medicine and ascended during the daytime in 363 A.D. In this book, Master Ni gives important details of Master Kou Hong's life and teaching which are of special interest to those engaged in spiritual cultivation and seeking spiritual benefit of life. 176 pages, Softcover, Stock No. BKOUH, $12.95.

Ageless Counsel for Modern Life - *New Publication!*
Master Ni's work entitled *The Book of Changes and the Unchanging Truth (I Ching)* contains sixty-four illustrative commentaries. Readers have found them meaningful and useful; they cover a variety of topics and give spiritual guidance for everyday life. Many readers requested the commentaries be printed apart from the big text, so we have put them all together in this one volume. The good directions and principles explained here can guide and enrich your life. Master Ni's delightful poetry and some teachings of esoteric Taoism can be found here as well. 256 pages, Softcover, Stock No. BAGEL, $15.95.

The Mystical Universal Mother - *New Publication!*
An understanding of both kinds of energies existing in the universe - masculine and feminine - are crucial to the understanding of oneself, in particular for people moving to higher spiritual evolution. In this book, Master Ni focuses upon the feminine as the Mystical Universal Mother and gives examples through the lives of some ancient and modern women, including a Taoist teacher known as Mother Chern or the Mother of Yellow Altar, some famous historical Chinese women, the first human woman called Neu Wu, and Master Ni's own mother. 240 pages, Softcover, Stock No. BMYST, $14.95

Moonlight in the Dark Night - *New Publication!*
In order to attain inner clarity and freedom of the soul, you have to get your emotions under control. It seems that spiritual achievement itself is not a great obstacle, once you understand what is helpful and what is not. What is left for most people is their own emotions, which affect the way they treat themselves and others. This will cause trouble for themselves or for other people. This book contains Taoist wisdom on the balancing of the emotions, including balancing love relationships, so that spiritual achievement can become possible. 168 pages, Softcover, Stock No. BMOON, $12.95

Harmony - The Art of Life - *New Publication!*
Harmony occurs when two different things find the point at which they can link together. The point of linkage, if healthy and helpful, brings harmony. Harmony is a spiritual matter which relates to each individual's personal sensitivity and sensitivity to each situation of daily life. Basically, harmony comes from understanding yourself. In this book, Master Ni shares some valuable Taoist understanding and insight about the ability to bring harmony within one's own self, one's relationships and the world. 208 pages, Stock No. BHARM, Softcover, $14.95

Attune Your Body with Dao-In: Taoist Exercise for a Long and Happy Life - *New Publication!* - Dao-In is a series of typical Taoist movements which are traditionally used for physical energy conducting. These exercises were passed down from the ancient achieved Taoists and immortals. The ancients discovered that Dao-In exercises not only solved problems of stagnant energy, but also increased their health and lengthened their years. The exercises are also used as practical support for cultivation and the higher achievements of spiritual immortality. 144 pages, STOCK NO. BDAOI, Softcover with photographs, $14.95

The Key to Good Fortune: Refining Your Spirit - *New Publication!* A translation of Straighten Your Way (Tai Shan Kan Yin Pien) and The Silent Way of Blessing (Yin Chia Wen), which are the main guidance for a mature and healthy life. This amplified version of the popular booklet called The Heavenly Way includes a new commentary section by Master Ni which discusses how spiritual improvement can be an integral part of one's life and how to realize a Heavenly life on earth. 144 pages, Stock No. BKEYT, Softcover, $12.95

Eternal Light - *New Publication!*
In this book, Master Ni presents the life and teachings of his father, Grandmaster Ni, Yo San, who was a spiritually achieved person, a Taoist healer and teacher, and a source of inspiration to Master Ni in his life. Here is an intimate look at the lifestyle of a spiritual family. Some of the deeper teachings and understandings of spirituality passed from father to son are clearly given and elucidated. This book is recommended for those committed to living a spiritual way of life and wishing for higher achievement. 208 pages, Stock No. BETER, Softcover, $14.95

Quest of Soul - *New Publication!*
In Quest of Soul, Master Ni addresses many subjects relevant to understanding one's own soul, such as the religious concept of saving the soul, how to improve the quality of the personal soul, the high spiritual achievement of free soul, what happens spiritually at death and the universal soul. He guides the reader into deeper knowledge of oneself and inspires each individual to move forward to increase one's own personal happiness and spiritual level. 152 pages, Stock No. BQUES, Softcover, $11.95

Nurture Your Spirits - *New Publication!*
With truthful spiritual knowledge, you have better life attitudes that are more supportive to your existence. With truthful spiritual knowledge, nobody can cause you spiritual confusion. Where can you find such advantage? It would take a lifetime of development in a correct school, but such a school is not available. However, in this book Master Ni breaks some spiritual prohibitions and presents the spiritual truth he has studied and proven. This truth may help you develop and nurture your own spirits which are the truthful internal foundation of your life being. The Integral Way is educational; its purpose is not to group people to build social strength but to help each individual build one's own spiritual strength. 176 pages, Stock No. BNURT, Softcover, $12.95

Internal Growth through Tao - *New Publication!*
Material goods can be passed from one person to another, but growth and awareness cannot be given in the same way. Spiritual development is related to one's own internal and external beingness. Through books, discussion or classes, wise people are able to use others' experiences to kindle their own inner light to help their own growth and live a life of no separation from their own spiritual nature. In this book, Master Ni teaches the more subtle, much deeper sphere of the reality of life that is above the shallow sphere of external achievement. He also shows the confusion caused by some spiritual teachings and guides you in the direction of developing spiritually by growing internally. 208 pages, Stock No. BINTE, Softcover, $13.95

Power of Natural Healing - *New Publication!*
Master Ni discusses the natural capability of self-healing in this book, which is healing physical trouble untreated by medication or external measure. He offers information and practices which can assist any treatment method currently being used by someone seeking health. He goes deeper to discuss methods of Taoist cultivation which promote a healthy life, including Taoist spiritual achievement, which brings about health and longevity. This book is not only suitable for a person seeking to improve their health condition. Those who wish to live long and happy lives, and to understand more about living a natural healthy lifestyle, may be supported by the practice of Taoist energy cultivation. 230 pages, Stock No. BHEAL, Softcover, $14.95

Essence of Universal Spirituality
In this volume, as an open-minded learner and achieved teacher of universal spirituality, Master Ni examines and discusses all levels and topics of religious and spiritual teaching to help you develop your own correct knowledge of the essence existing above the differences in religious practice. He reviews religious teachings with hope to benefit modern people. This book is to help readers to come to understand the ultimate truth and enjoy the

achievement of all religions without becoming confused by them. 304 pages, Stock No. BESSE, Softcover, $19.95

Guide to Inner Light
Modern life is controlled by city environments, cultural customs, religious teachings and politics that all can divert our attention away from our natural life being. As a result, we lose the perspective of viewing ourselves as natural completeness. This book reveals the development of ancient Taoist adepts. Drawing inspiration from their experience, modern people looking for the true source and meaning of life can find great teachings to direct and benefit them. The invaluable ancient Taoist development can teach us to reach the attainable spiritual truth and point the way to the Inner Light. Master Ni uses the ancient high accomplishments to make this book a useful resource. 192 pages, Stock No. BGUID, Softcover, $12.95

Stepping Stones for Spiritual Success
In Asia, the custom of foot binding was followed for close to a thousand years. In the West, people did not practice foot binding, but they bound their thoughts for a much longer period, some 1,500 to 1,700 years. Their mind and thinking became unnatural. Being unnatural expresses a state of confusion where people do not know what is right. Once they become natural again, they become clear and progress is great. Master Ni invites his readers to unbind their minds; in this volume, he has taken the best of the traditional teachings and put them into contemporary language to make them more relevant to our time, culture and lives. 160 pages, Stock No. BSTEP, Softcover, $12.95.

The Complete Works of Lao Tzu
Lao Tzu's Tao Teh Ching is one of the most widely translated and cherished works of literature in the world. It presents the core of Taoist philosophy. Lao Tzu's timeless wisdom provides a bridge to the subtle spiritual truth and practical guidelines for harmonious and peaceful living. Master Ni has included what is believed to be the only English translation of the Hua Hu Ching, a later work of Lao Tzu which has been lost to the general public for a thousand years. 212 pages, Stock No. BCOMP, Softcover, $12.95

Order The Complete Works of Lao Tzu and the companion Tao Teh Ching Cassette Tapes for only $23.00. Stock No. ABTAO.

The Book of Changes and the Unchanging Truth
The first edition of this book was widely appreciated by its readers, who drew great spiritual benefit from it. They found the principles of the I Ching to be clearly explained and useful to their lives, especially the helpful commentaries. The legendary classic I Ching is recognized as mankind's first written book of wisdom. Leaders and sages throughout history

have consulted it as a trusted advisor which reveals the appropriate action to be taken in any of life's circumstances. This volume also includes over 200 pages of background material on Taoist principles of natural energy cycles, instruction and commentaries. New, revised second edition, 669 pages, Stock No. BBOOK, Hardcover, $35.00

The Story of Two Kingdoms
This volume is the metaphoric tale of the conflict between the Kingdoms of Light and Darkness. Through this unique story, Master Ni transmits the esoteric teachings of Taoism which have been carefully guarded secrets for over 5,000 years. This book is for those who are serious in their search and have devoted their lives to achieving high spiritual goals. 122 pages, Stock No. BSTOR, Hardcover, $14.50

The Way of Integral Life
This book can help build a bridge for those wishing to connect spiritual and intellectual development. It is most helpful for modern educated people. It includes practical and applicable suggestions for daily life, philosophical thought, esoteric insight and guidelines for those aspiring to give help and service to the world. This book helps you learn the wisdom of the ancient sages' achievement to assist the growth of your own wisdom and integrate it as your own new light and principles for balanced, reasonable living in worldly life. 320 pages, Softcover, $14.00, Stock No. BWAYS. Hardcover, $20.00, Stock No. BWAYH

Enlightenment: Mother of Spiritual Independence
The inspiring story and teachings of Master Hui Neng, the father of Zen Buddhism and Sixth Patriarch of the Buddhist tradition, highlight this volume. Hui Neng was a person of ordinary birth, intellectually unsophisticated, who achieved himself to become a spiritual leader. Master Ni includes enlivening commentaries and explanations of the principles outlined by this spiritual revolutionary. Having received the same training as all Zen Masters as one aspect of his training and spiritual achievement, Master Ni offers this teaching so that his readers may be guided in their process of spiritual development. 264 pages, Softcover, $12.50, Stock No. BENLS. Hardcover, $22.00, Stock No. BENLH

Attaining Unlimited Life
The thought-provoking teachings of Chuang Tzu are presented in this volume. He was perhaps the greatest philosopher and master of Taoism and he laid the foundation for the Taoist school of thought. Without his work, people of later generations would hardly recognize the value of Lao Tzu's teaching in practical, everyday life. He touches the organic nature of human life more deeply and directly than do other great teachers. This volume also includes questions by students and answers by Master Ni. 467 pages, Softcover, $18.00, Stock No. BATTS; Hardcover, $25.00, Stock No. BATTH

Special Discount: Order the three classics Way of Integral Life, Enlightenment: Mother of Spiritual Independence *and* Attaining Unlimited Light *in the hardbound editions, Stock No.* BHARD *for $59.95.*

The Gentle Path of Spiritual Progress
This book offers a glimpse into the dialogues of a Taoist master and his students. In a relaxed, open manner, Master Ni, Hua-Ching explains to his students the fundamental practices that are the keys to experiencing enlightenment in everyday life. Many of the traditional secrets of Taoist training are revealed. His students also ask a surprising range of questions, and Master Ni's answers touch on contemporary psychology, finances, sexual advice, how to use the I Ching as well as the telling of some fascinating Taoist legends. 290 pages, Softcover, $12.95, Stock No. BGENT

Spiritual Messages from a Buffalo Rider, A Man of Tao
This is another important collection of Master Ni's service in his world trip, originally published as one half of The Gentle Path. He had the opportunity to meet people and answer their questions to help them gain the spiritual awareness that we live at the command of our animal nature. Our buffalo nature rides on us, whereas an achieved person rides the buffalo. In this book, Master Ni gives much helpful knowledge to those who are interested in improving their lives and deepening their cultivation so they too can develop beyond their mundane beings. 242 pages, Softcover, $12.95, Stock No. BSPIR

8,000 Years of Wisdom, Volume I and II
This two-volume set contains a wealth of practical, down-to-earth advice given by Master Ni to his students over a five-year period, 1979 to 1983. Drawing on his training in Traditional Chinese Medicine, Herbology, Acupuncture and other Taoist arts, Master Ni gives candid answers to students' questions on many topics ranging from dietary guidance to sex and pregnancy, meditation techniques and natural cures for common illnesses. Volume I includes dietary guidance; 236 pages; Stock No. BWIS1 Volume II includes sex and pregnancy guidance; 241 pages; Stock No. BWIS2. Softcover, each volume $12.50

Special discount: Both Books I and II of 8,000 Years of Wisdom, Stock No. BWIS3, for $22.00.

The Uncharted Voyage Toward the Subtle Light
Spiritual life in the world today has become a confusing mixture of dying traditions and radical novelties. People who earnestly and sincerely seek something more than just a way to fit into the complexities of a modern structure that does not support true self-development often find themselves spiritually struggling. This book provides a profound understanding and insight into the underlying heart of all paths of spiritual growth, the subtle origin and the eternal truth of one universal life. 424 pages. Stock No. BUNCH. Softcover, $14.50

The Heavenly Way
A translation of the classic Tai Shan Kan Yin Pien (Straighten Your Way) and Yin Chia Wen (The Silent Way of Blessing). The treatises in this booklet are the main guidance for a mature and healthy life. The purpose of this booklet is to promote the recognition of truth, because only truth can teach the perpetual Heavenly Way by which one reconnects oneself with the divine nature. 41 pages, Stock No. BHEAV, Softcover, $2.50

Special Discount: Order the Heavenly Way in a set of 10 - great for gifts or giveaways. (One shipping item). BHIV10 $17.50.

Footsteps of the Mystical Child
This book poses and answers such questions as: What is a soul? What is wisdom? What is spiritual evolution? The answers to these and many other questions enable readers to open themselves to new realms of understanding and personal growth. There are also many true examples about people's internal and external struggles on the path of self-development and spiritual evolution. 166 pages, Stock No. BFOOT, Softcover, $9.50

Workbook for Spiritual Development
This book offers a practical, down-to-earth, hands-on approach for those who are devoted to the path of spiritual achievement. The reader will find diagrams showing fundamental hand positions to increase and channel one's spiritual energy, postures for sitting, standing and sleeping cultivation as well as postures for many Taoist invocations. The material in this workbook is drawn from the traditional teachings of Taoism and summarizes thousands of years of little-known practices for spiritual development. An entire section is devoted to ancient invocations, another on natural celibacy and another on postures. In addition, Master Ni explains the basic attitudes and understandings that are the foundation for Taoist practices. 224 pages, Stock No. BWORK, Softcover, $12.50

Poster of Master Lu
Color poster of Master Lu, Tung Ping (shown on cover of workbook), for use with the workbook or in one's shrine. 16" x 22"; Stock No. PMLTP. $10.95

Order the Workbook for Spiritual Development *and the companion Poster of Master Lu for $18.95.* Stock No. BPWOR.

The Taoist Inner View of the Universe
This presentation of Taoist metaphysics provides guidance for one's own personal life transformation. Master Ni has given all the opportunity to know the vast achievement of the ancient unspoiled mind and its transpiercing vision. This book offers a glimpse of the inner

world and immortal realm known to achieved Taoists and makes it understandable for students aspiring to a more complete life. 218 pages, Stock No. BTAOI, Softcover, $14.95

Tao, the Subtle Universal Law
Most people are unaware that their thoughts and behavior evoke responses from the invisible net of universal energy. The real meaning of Taoist self-discipline is to harmonize with universal law. To lead a good stable life is to be aware of the actual conjoining of the universal subtle law with every moment of our lives. This book presents the wisdom and practical methods that the ancient Chinese have successfully used for centuries to accomplish this. 165 pages, Stock No. TAOS, Softcover, $7.50

MATERIALS ON TAOIST HEALTH, ARTS AND SCIENCES

BOOKS

101 Vegetarian Delights - *New Publication!*
A vegetarian diet is a gentle way of life with both physical and spiritual benefits, providing calmness, clear and supple skin, good health and vigorous well-being. The Oriental tradition provides helpful methods to assure that a vegetarian diet is well-balanced and nourishing. This book provides a variety of clear and precise recipes ranging from everyday nutrition to exotic and delicious feasts. Included are sections on Cooking with Herbs, Culinary Herb Gardens and Special Foods. 176 pages, Stock No. B101V, Softcover, $12.95

The Tao of Nutrition by Maoshing Ni, Ph.D., with Cathy McNease, B.S., M.H. - Working from ancient Chinese medical classics and contemporary research, the authors have compiled an indispensable guide to natural healing. This exceptional book shows how to control one's health through eating habits. This volume contains 3 major sections: the first deals with theories of Chinese nutrition and philosophy; the second describes over 100 common foods, listing their energetic properties, therapeutic actions and individual remedies. The third section lists nutritional remedies for common ailments. This book presents both a healing system and a disease prevention system flexible in adapting to each individual's needs. 214 pages, Stock No. BNUTR, Softcover, $14.50

Chinese Vegetarian Delights by Lily Chuang
An extraordinary collection of recipes based on principles of traditional Chinese nutrition. Many recipes are therapeutically prepared with herbs. Diet has long been recognized as a key factor in health and longevity. For those who require restricted diets and those who choose an optimal diet, this cookbook is a rare treasure. Meat, sugar, diary products and

fried foods are excluded. Produce, grains, tofu, eggs and seaweeds are imaginatively prepared. 104 pages. Stock No. BCHIV. Softcover, $7.50

Chinese Herbology Made Easy - by Maoshing Ni, Ph.D.
This text provides an overview of Oriental medical theory, in-depth descriptions of each herb category, over 300 black and white photographs, extensive tables of individual herbs for easy reference and an index of pharmaceutical and Pin-Yin names. The distillation of overwhelming material into essential elements provides an efficient focus and a clear understanding of Chinese herbology. This book is especially helpful for those studying for the California Acupuncture License. 202 pages. Stock No. BCHIH. Softcover, 14.50

Crane Style Chi Gong Book - By Daoshing Ni, Ph.D.
Chi Gong is a set of meditative exercises that was developed several thousand years ago by Taoists in China. It is now practiced for healing purposes, combining breathing techniques, body movements and mental imagery to guide the smooth flow of energy throughout the body. This book gives a more detailed account and study of Chi Gong than the videotape alone. It may be used with or without the videotape. Includes complete instructions and information on using Chi Gong exercise as a medical therapy. 55 pages. Stock No. BCRAN. Spiral-bound, $10.95

VIDEO TAPES

Attune Your Body with Dao-In: Taoist Physical Art for a Long and Happy Life (VHS) - by Master Ni. Dao-In is a series of typical Taoist movements which are traditionally used for conducting physical energy. These exercises were passed down from the ancient achieved Taoists and immortals. The ancients discovered that Dao-In exercises not only solved problems of stagnant energy, but also increased their health and lengthened their years. The exercises are also used as practical support for cultivation and the higher achievements of spiritual immortality. Master Ni, Hua-Ching, heir to the tradition of the achieved masters, is the first to release this important Taoist practice to the modern world in this 1-hour videotape. Stock No. VDAOI, VHS $59.95

T'ai Chi Ch'uan: An Appreciation (VHS) - by Master Ni.
Different styles of T'ai Chi Ch'uan as movement have different purposes and accomplish different results. In this long-awaited videotape, Master Ni, Hua-Ching presents three styles of T'ai Chi Movement handed down to him through generations of highly developed masters. They are the "Gentle Path," "Sky Journey" and "Infinite Expansion" styles of T'ai Chi Movement. The three styles are presented uninterrupted in this unique videotape and are set to music for observation and appreciation. Stock No. VAPPR. VHS 30 minutes $49.95

Crane Style Chi Gong (VHS) - by Dr. Daoshing Ni, Ph.D.
Chi Gong is a set of meditative exercises developed several thousand years ago by ancient Taoists in China. It is now practiced for healing stubborn chronic diseases, strengthening the body to prevent disease and as a tool for further spiritual enlightenment. It combines breathing techniques, simple body movements, and mental imagery to guide the smooth flow of energy throughout the body. Chi Gong is easy to learn for all ages. Correct and persistent practice will increase one's energy, relieve stress or tension, improve concentration and clarity, release emotional stress and restore general well-being. 2 hours, Stock No. VCRAN. $65.95

Eight Treasures (VHS) - By Maoshing Ni, Ph.D.
These exercises help open blocks in your energy flow and strengthen your vitality. It is a complete exercise combining physical stretching and toning and energy-conducting movements coordinated with breathing. The Eight Treasures are an exercise unique to the Ni family. Patterned from nature, its 32 movements are an excellent foundation for T'ai Chi Ch'uan or martial arts. 1 hour, 45 minutes. Stock No. VEIGH. $49.95

T'ai Chi Ch'uan I & II (VHS) - By Maoshing Ni, Ph.D.
This exercise integrates the flow of physical movement with that of internal energy in the Taoist style of "Harmony," similar to the long form of Yang-style T'ai Chi Ch'uan. Tai Chi has been practiced for thousands of years to help both physical longevity and spiritual cultivation. 1 hour each. Each video tape $49.95. Order both for $90.00. Stock Nos: Part I, VTAI1; Part II, VTAI2; Set of two, VTAI3.

AUDIO CASSETTES

Invocations for Health and Longevity and Healing a Broken Heart - By Maoshing Ni, Ph.D. *Updated with additional material!* This audio cassette guides the listener through a series of ancient invocations to channel and conduct one's own healing energy and vital force. "Thinking is louder than thunder." The mystical power which creates all miracles is your sincere practice of this principle. 30 minutes, Stock No. AINVO, $9.95

Stress Release with Chi Gong - By Maoshing Ni, Ph.D.
This audio cassette guides you through simple, ancient breathing exercises that enable you to release day-to-day stress and tension that are such a common cause of illness today. 30 minutes. Stock No. ACHIS. $9.95

Pain Management with Chi Gong - By Maoshing Ni, Ph.D.
Using easy visualization and deep-breathing techniques that have been developed over thousands of years, this audio cassette offers methods for overcoming pain by invigorating your energy flow and unblocking obstructions that cause pain. 30 minutes, Stock No. ACHIP. $9.95

Tao Teh Ching Cassette Tapes
This classic work of Lao Tzu has been recorded in this two-cassette set that is a companion to the book translated by Master Ni. Professionally recorded and read by Robert Rudelson. 120 minutes. Stock No. ATAOT. $12.95

Order Master Ni's book, *The Complete Works of Lao Tzu,* and Tao Teh Ching Cassette Tapes for only $23.00. Stock No. ABTAO.

This list of Master Ni's books in English is ordered by date of publication for those readers who wish to follow the sequence of his Western teaching material in their learning of Tao.

1979: *The Complete Works of Lao Tzu*
The Taoist Inner View of the Universe
Tao, the Subtle Universal Law

1983: *The Book of Changes and the Unchanging Truth*
8,000 Years of Wisdom, I
8,000 Years of Wisdom, II

1984: *Workbook for Spiritual Development*

1985: *The Uncharted Voyage Toward the Subtle Light*

1986: *Footsteps of the Mystical Child*

1987: *The Gentle Path of Spiritual Progress*
Spiritual Messages from a Buffalo Rider (originally part of *Gentle Path of Spiritual Progress*)

1989: *The Way of Integral Life*
Enlightenment: Mother of Spiritual Independence
Attaining Unlimited Life
The Story of Two Kingdoms

1990: *Stepping Stones for Spiritual Success*
Guide to Inner Light
Essence of Universal Spirituality

1991: *Internal Growth through Tao*
Nurture Your Spirits
Quest of Soul
Power of Natural Healing
Attune Your Body with Dao-In: Taoist Exercise for a Long and Happy Life
Eternal Light
The Key to Good Fortune: Refining Your Spirit

1992: *Harmony: The Art of Life*
Moonlight in the Dark Night
Life and Teachings of Two Immortals, Volume I: Kou Hong
The Mystical Universal Mother
Ageless Counsel for Modern Times
Gentle Path T'ai Chi Ch'uan
Taoist Mysticism: The Uniting of God and Human Life

In addition, the forthcoming books will be compiled from his lecturing and teaching service:

Golden Message: The Essence of Your Daily Life (by Daoshing and Maoshing Ni, based on the works of Master Ni, Hua-Ching)
Sky Journey T'ai Chi Ch'uan
Infinite Expansion T'ai Chi Ch'uan
Cosmic Tour Ba Gua Zahn
Life and Teachings of Two Immortals, Volume II: Chen Tuan
Internal Alchemy: An Introduction to Immortality
Esoteric Tao Teh Ching: Its Relevance Illuminated

How To Order

Name: _____

Address: _____

City: _____ State: _____ Zip: _____

Phone - Daytime: _____ Evening: _____

(We may telephone you if we have questions about your order.)

Qty.	Stock No.	Title/Description	Price Each	Total Price

Total amount for items ordered _____

Sales tax (CA residents only, 8-1/4%) _____

Shipping Charge (see below) _____

Total Amount Enclosed _____

Visa _____ Mastercard _____ Expiration Date _____

Card number: _____

Signature: _____

Shipping: In the US, we use UPS when possible. Please give full street address or nearest crossroads. All packages are insured at no extra charge. If shipping to more than one address, use separate shipping charges. Remember: 1 - 10 copies of Heavenly Way, Tao Teh Ching audiotape set and each book and tape are single items. Posters (up to 5 per tube) are a separate item. Please allow 2 - 4 weeks for US delivery and 6 - 10 weeks for foreign surface mail.

By Mail: Complete this form with payment (US funds only, No Foreign Postal Money Orders, please) and mail to: Union of Tao and Man, 1314 Second St. #A, Santa Monica, CA 90401

Phone Orders: (310) 576-1901 - You may leave credit card orders anytime on our answering machine. Please speak clearly and remember to leave your full name and daytime phone number. We will call only if we have a question with your order, there is a delay or you specifically ask for phone confirmation.

Inquiries: If you have questions concerning your order, please refer to the date and invoice number on the top center of your invoice to help us locate your order swiftly.

Shipping Charges -
  Domestic Surface: First item $3.25, each additional, add $.50.
  Canada Surface: First item $3.25, each additional, add $1.00.
  Canada Air: First item $4.00, each additional, add $2.00.
  Foreign Surface: First Item $3.50, each additional, add $2.00.
  Foreign Air: First item $12.00, each additional, add $7.00.

For the Trade: Wholesale orders may be placed direct to publisher, or with NewLeaf, BookPeople, The Distributors, Inland Books, GreatWay or Quality Books in US; DeepBooks in Europe; Quest Book Trade Distributors in Australia.

Thank you for your order

Spiritual Study through the College of Tao

The College of Tao and the Union of Tao and Man were established formally in California in the 1970's. This tradition is a very old spiritual culture of mankind, holding long experience of human spiritual growth. Its central goal is to offer healthy spiritual education to all people of our society. This time-tested tradition values the spiritual development of each individual self and passes down its guidance and experience.

Master Ni carries his tradition from its country of origin to the west. He chooses to avoid making the mistake of old-style religions that have rigid establishments which resulted in fossilizing the delicacy of spiritual reality. He prefers to guide the teachings of his tradition as a school of no boundary rather than a religion with rigidity. Thus, the branches or centers of this Taoist school offer different programs of similar purpose. Each center extends its independent service, but all are unified in adopting Master Ni's work as the foundation of teaching to fulfill the mission of providing spiritual education to all people.

The centers offer their classes, teaching, guidance and practices on building the groundwork for cultivating a spiritually centered and well-balanced life. As a person obtains the correct knowledge with which to properly guide himself or herself, he or she can then become more skillful in handling the experiences of daily life. The assimilation of good guidance in one's practical life brings about different stages of spiritual development.

Any interested individual is welcome to join and learn to grow for yourself. Or you just might like to take a few classes in which you are interested. You might like to visit the center or take classes near where you live, or you may be interested in organizing a center or study group based on the model of existing centers. In that way, we all work together for the spiritual benefit of all people. We do not require any religious type of commitment.

The College of Tao also offers a Self-Study program based on Master Ni's books and videotapes. The course outline and details of how to participate are given in his book, *The Golden Message*. The Self-Study program gives people an opportunity to study the learning of Tao at their own speed, for those who wish to study on their own or are too far from a center.

The learning is life. The development is yours. The connection of study may be helpful, useful and serviceable, directly to you.

- -

Mail to: Union of Tao and Man, 1314 Second Street #A, Santa Monica, CA 90401

_____ I wish to be put on the mailing list of the Union of Tao and Man to be notified of classes, educational activities and new publications.

Name:_____

Address:_____

City:_____State:_____Zip:_____

Herbs Used by Ancient Taoist Masters

The pursuit of everlasting youth or immortality throughout human history is an innate human desire. Long ago, Chinese esoteric Taoists went to the high mountains to contemplate nature, strengthen their bodies, empower their minds and develop their spirit. From their studies and cultivation, they gave China alchemy and chemistry, herbology and acupuncture, the I Ching, astrology, martial arts and T'ai Chi Ch'uan, Chi Gong and many other useful kinds of knowledge.

Most important, they handed down in secrecy methods for attaining longevity and spiritual immortality. There were different levels of approach; one was to use a collection of food herb formulas that were only available to highly achieved Taoist masters. They used these food herbs to increase energy and heighten vitality. This treasured collection of herbal formulas remained within the Ni family for centuries.

Now, through Traditions of Tao, the Ni family makes these foods available for you to use to assist the foundation of your own positive development. It is only with a strong foundation that expected results are produced from diligent cultivation.

As a further benefit, in concert with the Taoist principle of self-sufficiency, Traditions of Tao offers the food herbs along with the Union of Tao and Man's publications in a distribution opportunity for anyone serious about financial independence.

Send to: *Traditions of Tao*
               1314 Second Street #A
               Santa Monica, CA 90401

☐ *Please send me a Traditions of Tao brochure.*

☐ *Please send me information on becoming an independent distributor of Traditions of Tao herbal products and publications.*

Name _____

*Address*_____

*City*_____*State*_____*Zip*_____

*Phone (day)*_____*(night)*_____

Yo San University of Traditional Chinese Medicine

"Not just a medical career, but a life-time commitment to raising one's spiritual standard."

Thank you for your support and interest in our publications and services. It is by your patronage that we continue to offer you the practical knowledge and wisdom from this venerable Taoist tradition.

Because of your sustained interest in Taoism, in January 1989 we formed Yo San University of Traditional Chinese Medicine, a non-profit educational institute under the direction of founder Master Ni, Hua-Ching. Yo San University is the continuation of 38 generations of Ni family practitioners who handed down knowledge and wisdom from father to son. Its purpose is to train and graduate practitioners of the highest caliber in Traditional Chinese Medicine, which includes acupuncture, herbology and spiritual development.

We view Traditional Chinese Medicine as the application of spiritual development. Its foundation is the spiritual capability to know life, to know a person's problem and how to cure it. We teach students how to care for themselves and others, and emphasize the integration of traditional knowledge and modern science. We offer a complete Master's degree program approved by the California State Department of Education that provides an excellent education in Traditional Chinese Medicine and meets all requirements for state licensure.

We invite you to inquire into our school for a creative and rewarding career as a holistic physician. Classes are also open to persons interested only in self-enrichment. For more information, please fill out the form below and send it to:

Yo San University
1314 Second Street
Santa Monica, CA 90401

☐ Please send me information on the Masters degree program in Traditional Chinese Medicine.

☐ Please send me information on health workshops and seminars.

☐ Please send me information on continuing education for acupuncturists and health professionals.

Name _____

Address _____

City_____State_____Zip_____

Phone(day)_____(night)_____

Index of Some Topics

(19)

Yin = lead
Yang = mercury

(19) Energy Child Birth
Golden Boy
Jade Girl
Yellow Lady = Earth